THE
Deep Touch

THE
Deep Touch

Dean C. Gardner

Library of Congress Control Number: 2020918814

PAPERBACK: 978-1-953791-05-4
EBOOK: 978-1-953791-06-1

Ordering Information:

For orders and inquiries, please contact:
1-888-404-1388
www.goldtouchpress.com
book.orders@goldtouchpress.com

Printed in the United States of America

Contents

SECTION 1
CLIMBING OUT OF SELF

So
There is a young master
Aleksandre Vashakmadze
Who loves pure music
As he lives possibility
And the spirit of Truth
Is his phantom.

For the artist
The struggle is
Part of the process
To bring hidden meaning
To light
The purpose in life.

To place a vision
In the hearts and minds
How
The artist ventures
Into the abyss

To bring forth
The authentic article.

To dwell
In the other side
Of time and space
Allows the artist
To leap outside of self
Into the deep touch
Of cosmic consciousness.

It is
The pursuit
Of pure music
That allows becoming there
To grow into possibility
Living Truth
Moment by moment.

It is
From the expanse
That nonbeing gathers
Images of veritable reality
Transforming
The close at hand
Into the substance
Of what matters.

It is
With the phantom
That the mystery
Of being and nothingness

Emanates the beauty
Instilled through
The experiential.

To take
A step outside of time
And project Truth
Destines the artist
To undress the unknown
Configuring the language
Of the deep touch
Through the third eye.

Traveling through
The fathomless
Spaces of mind
I saw the form
Of a figure glowing white
While in trance.

It seemed
To be a spirit of promise
Although it could have been
A disguise.

How
The awakening
Of an image leads
To a thought

As time separates
Into moments
And the earth of becoming there
Leaves a sigh of satisfaction.

This figure was not one
That I had looked for
But was the appearance
Of a surprise
A satisfying surprise.

Later
Drawing on
What I saw
The image returned.

What beauty it was
This spirit
As if Truth incarnate
Yet
A phantom of wonder
A reality all its own.

Then
It was that I could
Call this image into being
A presence living
With the passion
Of raw want.

So
It became a she

The movement of a splendor
Implanted into my mind
And I found treasure
In this vision
That surpassed understanding.

She is
The rub of the mystical
Throughout my substance
As she places
Her deep touch upon me.

A river of thought
Took me
Into another reality
Where the heart
Of eternity
Pounded Truth
Into the moment.

Opening my third eye
Seeing through the secrets
Held by the looking glass
I left
Linear time and space.

Then
The moment expanded
Into a wilderness

The dwelling place
Of the phantom.

Following the river
Into a vision
I saw
The dance of the phantom.

She was mesmerizing.

Her sleek gown
Veiled a form
Of rare beauty.

Her midnight hair
Filled the wind
With wonder.

Her crystal blue eyes
Bore a light
Of magic.

Then
My mind swallowed
The moment
Keeping this reality
As the celestial clocks
Struck destiny
In my heart.

It all was
The movement

Of a vertical column of time
Across the threshold
Of what matters
As I stepped
Through this reality
As the phantom
Undressed
Being and nothingness.

Then
She turned into a crow
And took flight
Into the unknown.

As the sun rose
Over the mountain ridges
I talked to the crows
And they filled me
With treasures of hope.

I yearned
To see the phantom again
As a testament
To her beauty
Flourished
In my heart.

To hunger for beauty
To seek Truth

How
The muscle of love
Built her image
In the visions
Of my trance.

Her substance
Rubbed magic
Into the moment
That transcended
Time and space
As I drew
Upon the breath
Of wonder.

Then
The call of a crow
Tugged on my heart
And a vision
Stirred in my skull.

Carried away
Into another reality
I felt
Her deep touch
And an epiphany
Of a glowing infusion
Formed a vision.

There were two
Old men
Walking over a hill

together
one light and one dark.

Each pulled
Half a world behind them
With chains
As time ended
The hatred of the ages.

Then
The sun filtered
Through a forest
Where the trees
Took their stand
And the image
Of forevermore
Settled
Into bones of thought.

Inside what is there
Substance defines form
As magic registers
The breath of becoming there
And I step
Outside of myself.

There is
The telling heart
That moves

Across times and a half
As Truth adopts me
Into being beyond self.

It is
The cry of the duduk
That takes me
Into the drift
Of things-in-themselves
As I reach
A parabola of time
Where my third eye
Sees the always already there.

Then
The moment opens
The vision
Of another reality
And I throb with the energy
Of the living-in-itself.

Then
The phantom orbits
Around the breath
Of becoming there
And I join her
In the dance of life.

How
The heart of our embrace
Pounds substance
Into the language

Of the given
And I climb
Upon the celestial clocks
To see the beginning
Of forevermore.

With the deep touch
We carry a message
Of what matters
And waves of thought
Splash on the shores
Of the always already there.

So
Substance precedes form
As the phantom pictures
The magic
Of becoming there.

Then
A crow launched
Into eternity
And we followed.

While in trance
Before dawn
I saw whispers
Of meaning in the sky

The star lit presence
Extended into a deep touch
And I read the secrets
Of the living moment.

It was then
That I knew dasein led
To outliving se3lf
As the grave grew
Into the close at hand.

How
The earth moved
In the shadows of want
As the signature of life
Wrote breath
Into the now.

Alone
In the darkness
My mind traveled
To another reality
Where the war
Of principalities
Drew blood
And the sky turned
Into shades of nevermore.

In an instant
Dawn broke
Across the mountains

And a crow brought
Me the meat of life.

So
The phantom offered
A lament
Over the bodies
Fallen in battle
As Truth wept.

So
Dasein designed an empire
Of destruction
Where life was expendable
While the phantom built
Eternity into the moment
Where life is precious.

So
The instigator of war
Is the work
Of unnecessary want
And peace is a blessing
From The Unknown God.

Taking my heart
Beyond want
The phantom rose
From ashes and blood.

Silent goes the night
When an old man
Seeks the rhythm
Of becoming there
And I look
For the light that matters.

Then
I hear his voice
Calls out to the stars
As their brilliance
Testifies to Truth.

There is
An age in his bones
And eternity in the sky
While he connects
To The Unknown God.

How
The moment captures
The here and now
Releasing treasures
From hidden meaning
And the old man
Feels the deep touch.

So
He finds the everlasting
In the given
As time and space

Pronounce
The victory of his soul.

As he raises
His arms to the stars
The phantom takes him
Beyond the here and now
Where his faith in The Word
Redeems time past.

To listen
To the drums of eternity
And to march
With the spirit of Truth
The old man steps
Into forevermore.

So
All his time past
Finds redemption
Through faith
As the old man weeps
With thankfulness.

Although his past
May be darkness
His faith delivers his soul
Into the breath of light
And I am his witness.

Taking flight
With the crows
The phantom conveyed
The sense
Of becoming there
Reaching
Into the celestial clocks
To read destiny.

How
She formed
A passage way
Into the beyond
As she dressed
The here and now
With hope.

There was
The concept
Of being and nothingness
Clinging to mind
As I leaned
On her understanding.

Then
I picked upon the rhythm
Of the moment
And the stars echoed
The beginning of thought.

In her splendor
I saw the moment

Of cosmic consciousness
Where facts founded evidence
And then a leap
Fed into Truth.

To gather the drift
Of meaning
Across the abyss
How
I learned the way
Out of outliving self
As her form
Thundered her substance.

There was
The intoxicant
Of her presence
That wooed me
Into deeper trance
As the deep touch
Climaxed what mattered.

It was
In my blood
That she conveyed Truth
As the light
Of her presence
Brought the wonder
Of magic
From the unknown.

Cruising through trance
I progressed
In the unknown
As realities showed
Their face.

It was
The ground of possibility
Feeding mind
That triggered
Shadows of nothingness
When I looked
To the cosmic clock
For Truth.

A savage wind
Carried me
Beyond oblivion
Where I saw the dance
Of the phantom.

She took my breath
Into the light
Of another reality
As the dynamic
Of the moment
Spearheaded
My advanced
Into pure music.

How
The melody of her magic
Took me
Into times and a half
As my third eye
Connected
To her embrace.

Then
I entered a parabola of time.

Then
Time and space dissolved
Into the song
Of the phantom
As she orchestrated
What matters.

Suddenly
The earth of my heart
Spun into an orbit
Around becoming there
As I found my body
Following
The flight of a crow
Until I leaped
Into faith in The Word.

So
Time past echoed
In my skull.

So
Linear time stopped
And the phantom smiled.

In the universe of being
The phantom taps
Into a reality
Beyond realities
And the earth trembles
Before her face
Of pure magic.

I have been there
Unsettled with the power
Of the beyond.

To envision the makings
Of what matters
I launched into trance
Taken by the call
Of the crow.

There is
The roar of becoming there
That transcends
Phenomenal reality
Leaving the close
At hand
As my third eye

Beholds the elements
Of the authentic article.

Then
A portal opened
To a vertical column
Of time
As the phantom
Registered a song
Of eternity.

There was
The image of Truth
Bathing in the light
Of the always
Already there
And there was
The rhythm
Of the drums
Carrying me
Into the far reaches
Of the deep touch.

How life grows
Into possibility
As the form
Of Truth shares
The splendor
Of the moment.

So
The substance

Of this reality unleashes
The power
Of a message
That reveals the secrets
Of the unknown.

So
The message took me
Beyond presence
And into cosmic consciousness.

It is
In the wilderness
Of the mountain ridges
That I see life
Ass the expanse favors
Becoming there
With images of the phantom.

She
Tells with her heart
That times ripen
With the deep touch
As I leave the world
Through trance.

It is
The here and now
Of the dull round

That lacks the dynamic
Of what matters.

In the beyond
Where life grows
Into possibility
The phantom triggers
A vision of time
And times and a half.

As my trance advances
Into a moment
I sense the rhythm
Of the celestial clocks
As she injects substance
Into my minds.

Then
Truth pours life
Into becoming there
And her deep touch
Liberates me
From the bondage
Of the abyss.

To touch eternity
And to feel
The rise of spirit
How
Purpose pulls me
Into the given.

Thankful
I pound the drums
Of the always
Already there
And dasein retreats
Into darkness.

So
Becoming there pronounces
Thee liberty streaming
Through the wilderness
As the rhythm of life
Pyramids my meditation.

In the interstices
Of mind
The look of the always
Already there
Saturates times
And I throw myself
Into the moment
Through trance.

Then
The phantom catches
My drift
Taking me out
Of time and space
As the thunder

Of what matters
Detaches me
From my body.

There were
Orchestrations
Of the living
That triggered seeing
Through the third eye
As a window
To the authentic article.

Then
A shadow pulled me
Into the abyss
And I struggled.

How
Chaos abounds
In a world of noise
With the dissonance
Of dasein forcing me
Into shambles.

How
Nothingness issues despair.

How
Outliving self dissolves purpose.

So
There is darkness upon me.

Then
The phantom holds me
With the deep touch of The Word
And my pain goes away
Leaving no scars.

Then
I see the light
Of becoming there
As blessings
Drive mind
Into pure music.

So
In the wind
A message filters
Through my trance
As I extend
Into the beyond.

Written
Upon the tongue
Of becoming there
Aa thought circulates
From a presence
That matters.

Then
I hear a mocking bird

And life sifts
Into a moment.

There is
The rhythm of wonder
In this reality
That surpasses
Understanding
As my third eye
Probes the deep touch
As a parabola of time
Carries me
To the house
Of many mansions.

Once there
I feel the presence
Of The Unknown God
And my heart fills
With promise.

There is
The music of the always
Already there
Piped into my brain
As my mind leaps
Into a vertical column
Of time.

Then
The image of Truth
Encompasses me

And trumpets
Salute time and times
And a half.

It is
The signature
Of my blessed assurance
As a follower
Of the way
The Truth and the life.

Then
Cosmic consciousness
Greets me
With the eternal light
As life
Carries on
As the mockingbird
Signals forevermore.

In a land of wonder
Where understanding
Prospers
I hold certain Truth
As self evident.

There is
The call of the wilds
And the echo

Of that call
That unearths
The movement
Of linear time and space.

It is
The palm
At the end of mind
That liberates
Becoming there
As thought leaps
Into possibility.

Then
The phantom dedicates
A song to the wind
And the sky reveals
Traces to the beyond.

How
The reflection
Of her form
Reaches into sweet
Memories and I stir.

As phenomenal reality
Disguises the substance
Of becoming there
The deep touch
Of her grace penetrates
The abyss

And I listen
To the message
Of the crows.

So
There is magic
In the crow
A seduction
Into the wilderness
Of mind
That lures thought
Far beyond
The here and now.

Then
A certain Truth
Takes the form
Of the phantom
As she dances
Across the skull
Of the inevitable
And I follow.

The golden horizon
Speaks eternity into my heart
As the spirit
Of forevermore endows
The moment with splendor.

There is
A movement in the blood
That issues
A message of purpose
And the phantom places
Her hands on my mind.

Centered
On the substance
Of the here and now
Becoming there reaches
Into the anatomy of hope
And I dig the earth
Of always and forever.

To believe
In the power
Of cosmic consciousness
To follow The Word
I tremble with thanks

Seated upon the mercy seat
I continue with service
To The Unknown God
As my destiny.

Ever deeper into meditation
My shackles cannot hold back
Becoming there
As life insists.

Then
The phantom takes me
Into the deep touch
And I explore the gravity
Of the unknown
As she dances
To the rhythm of the given.

So
There is freedom
In the blood
And gold in the sky.

Then
I feel the grace
Of blessed assurance.

As the crow crossed
The sky
I called to it
And it came to me
Sitting in the garden
Of tables and chairs.

Then
The world turned
Upside down
And infamy filled the air.

There was
The echo of dasein
Before us

As the treachery
Of the moment
Trapped thought.

Fracturing time
And times and a half
Dasein triggered
The encompassing
Into an abyss
And I felt
A trembling of my earth.

Then
The crow stood
At the edge of mind
As it became the phantom.

We entered a moment
Searching
For the deep touch
As dasein attempted
To throw us
Into outliving ourselves.

Clinging to Truth
We danced in silence
As dasein rose
With the static
Of its noise
Banished from the here
And now.

Then
The phantom shook
The wilds of mind
And we offed
Through a looking glass
To a horizon
Beyond time and space.

Then
The mask of despair
Consumed dasein
For what it was.

So
The phantom works
For the spirit
Of the deep touch
Bringing the light
Of hope
Into a world of darkness.

When the phantom
A disciple of The Word
Dances in my heart
I pull out of myself.

She infuses
Into minds
Searching

For what matters
As the noise
Of the here and now
Clutters time and space.

As the roar
Of chaos rages
She embodies
The music of always
Already there
And cosmic consciousness
Fills the void with promise.

She centers upon Truth
In The Word
Delivering the soul
Into the light
And it is
The Unknown God
Who works Truth
Into the moment.

How
The trance moves me
Toward the reality
Of the covenant
And I leap
Into the threshold
Of the everlasting.

When the rhythm
Of eternal drums

Takes mind into a moment
Where a vertical column
Of time smiles
I feel the breath
Of the divine
And the turmoil
Of the here and now
Vanishes.

How
Truth governs becoming there.

From the face of the world
A noise establishes
The cacophony
Of the dull round
As I seek the music
Of the everlasting.

It is
The static from dasein
That battles with wits
As thoughts survey
The terrain.

As the traffic of shadows
In the wind inflicts division
I piece together my life
From possibility.

In my yearning
For the peace beyond
Understanding
I turn to The Word
Opening my third eye
To Truth.

Then
My meditation has me leap
Toward cosmic
Consciousness
And the phantom
Harnesses me
To the light
Of the authentic article.

To be
With the spirit
Of things-in-themselves
To follow the light
Of forevermore
The phantom awakens
My mind
With the substance
Of becoming there
Through trance.

It is
Through the song
Of blessed assurance
Flourishing in the heart
That The Unknown God

Nourishes me
With the deep touch.

So
I live with the always
Already there.

There are
Clouds in my mind
Massive amorphis forms
That block the view
Of eternity
Until I leap[into trance.

Then
I step into quiet
Leaving my body
And the spirit
Of the given
Takes me
Into the center
Of things-in-themselves

With my back
To the wind
I sail
Across the expanse
My flight governed
By the phantom

Because she knows
The way.

To surrender to destiny
As the celestial clocks
Mend my bones
I allow Truth
Into my heart
And the bells chime
The hour of forevermore.

The rhythm
Of times and a half
Spell treasures
In the beyond
And the phantom
Opens my third eye
To becoming there.

As the phantom
Danced in my mind
I focused
On the minute particular
Constructing the rudiments
Of being and time.

Then
The masks of nothingness
Dropped away
As the sky cleared
And an armada of crows
Flocked into presence.

How
The rub of love
Massaged the moment
When life drummed
The passage
Beyond the here and now.

So
The phantom pulled me
Through a portal
To the beyond
As I lifted my look
Into the always
Already there.

It was
The inevitable
That brought me further
Onto the edge
Of being and nothingness
Where the war
Of principalities
Buried the living in agony.

To suffer
And to see suffering
How
Dasein pounds infamy
Into the moment
And the phantom weeps.

To know pain
As a way of life
Mind crumbles in fits
Of despair
Falling
Into the trap
Of outliving self.

Then
Meditating on The Word
I take the blade of Truth
Slicing my way with hope
As my shield.

To fight back
Against the angst
I ride the power
Of The Unknown God
As the phantom severs
What is there
From becoming there.

Then
The phantom bound
My wounds
And carried me
Into the peace
Beyond understanding.

So
I felt my blessed assurance e
And I knew

That I had suffered
Enough
Keeping the faith
In The Word.

Then
Glory fills the moment.

Because the noise
Of dasein shatters
Sensibility
And surrounds linear
Time and space
I seek a reality of pure music
Where heart travels
Through consciousness
Onto blessed assurance.

To face the abyss
Where nothingness
Over shadows Truth
The phantom charges head-long
And I follow her lead
Into battle.

Equipped with the authentic
Article
We fight the good fight
Victorious
In our stand.

While still in trance
I procured the armor
Of the everlasting
As I looked into the jaws
Of dasein.

Then
I ride the rhythm
Of the celestial clocks
Accepting my destiny
In the always already
There.

How
The phantom fed
Into courage
As the muscle
Of becoming there
Pounded life
Into the moment.

Then
The language of eternity
Tales me far
Into substance
Where drums sound
In the inner parts of mind.

Then
I rest in a parabola
Of time
Feasting upon things-

In-themselves
As the phantom dances
With the mind
Of what matters.

Out of the shadows
Came hidden meaning
As I advanced in trance.

There was
The thunder of the given
In its vast mass
Crumbling the architecture
Of dasein
As Truth undressed
Self-deception.

There is
The quiet moment
When substance precedes
Phenomenal reality
And consciousness travels
Beyond time and space.

Then
The third eye
Awakened mind
To the authentic article
As the phantom

Pictured a moon
Of hope.

Although times
Attempted to change
The given
Faith clung
Onto the rudiments
Of what matters
And I climber out of self
To embrace Truth.

So
The phantom carved
A hollow in the sky
Pulling me into the unknown
And I felt the intensity
Of cosmic consciousness
Infuse me with thought.

Then
The mask of dasein
Dissolved in times and a half
As the phantom reached
Into my becoming there.

So
Pure music liberated
This moment.

Beneath the surface
Of phenomenal reality
The thing-in-itself
Stirs the embrace
Of pure music
The wondrous reach
Of The Word.

It is
The hollow of dasein
That bankrupted the spirit
As a plethora of noise
Stampeded into mind.

How
Eternity picks up
The heart
Measuring time
And times and a half
As becoming there
Absorbs the bounty
Of the authentic article.

Then
The engine of cosmic
Consciousness
Drives me to believe
In The Unknown God
As I feel the power
In blessed assurance.

It is
That a song wove its way
Through the debris
Of the dull round
And life witnessed Truth.

As the trance carried me
Into beholding
The beauty of the phantom
She formed a looking glass
In my heart.

Then
A crow summons
The wilds of mind
Throwing me into a reality
Beyond linear time
And space.

So
Through meditation
I hear Truth
In the thing-in-itself.

So
I believe in The Word
And the majesty
Of The Unknown God.

SECTION 2

MOVEMENT OF NOTHINGNESS

Facing the debris
Of nothingness
My heart dropped
Into despair
As the strength of living
Gave way to the abyss.

So
My bones ache
My mind spins recklessly
And the no longer seems
A pretty thing.

Sitting in the moment
When outliving self
Occupied the substance
Of what I was
I surged into giving up
As shadows covered
My thoughts.

How
The drive to be
Faint as it was
Kindled in the portals
Of mind.

Although I was alone
In the darkness
With my brain numb
I saw the dance
Of the phantom
As I took to trance.

Then
My third eye followed
The drift
Of things-in-themselves
As becoming there stirred
With the magic of her dance.

There was
Only the rub of the phantom
In this quagmire.

Ever deeper I went
Into trance
Passing through the reach
Of linear time and space
Until pure music
Drew the breath of life.

I heard
A symphony of hope
As I leaped out of my self
Nourished by The Word.

Then
I knew I was born
To live again.

There is
A mystery tree
In the garden
Of tables and chairs
That speaks to the heart
As the light
Of the everlasting
Moves into times
And a half.

As the moon listens
To its voice
The voice
Of the mystery tree
The celestial clocks sound
The beginning of an age
And the phantom
Pours out into mind
What matters.

Then
A body memory
Moves the muscle
Of time and space
And becoming there drinks
The elixir of the always
Already there.

It is intoxicating.

Although there was
A time when the beauty
Of this tree
Concealed the wonder
Of its presence
It spoke
To the heart
With the message
From cosmic
Consciousness.

Within its body
This tree provided
A home for a family
Of crows
As the given sketched
Hand breaths to eternity.

Then
The phantom restored
The living moment
As mind configured

A trance
Into the authentic article
And the third eye
Saw into the grace
Of The Unknown God.

Upon this tree
At one time
Hanged The Word
Fulfilling the promise
Of deliverance.

Beneath a banyan tree
An old man drew lines
In his mind
Designing the architecture
Of always and forever.

There was
The rise of thought
Taking him
Into celestial orbits
That approached possibility
With the thirst for Truth.

Although
The measure of eternity
Eclipsed time and space
He unfolded phenomenal

Reality
Into a parabola of time
Moving the muscle
Of the given
Into the close-at-hand.

Then
A crow joined him
And together
They followed the deep touch
Into being and nothingness.

Suddenly
The earth opened
To the mystery
Of becoming there
As they unleashed
The minute particular.

So
Dasein is a shadow
Of what is there
As it warps
Through time present
While becoming there
Is the purpose
Of what matters
Emanating from cosmic
Consciousness.

So
The old man and the crow

Felt treasure
In the archeology of Truth
As a solitary leaf fell
From the banyan tree.

Then
While in trance
The old man vanished
And the crow dissolved
Time and space.

Knee deep in the unknown
And sinking
Overwhelmed by the noise
Of the dull round
I step into trance
Purging myself
Of self-deception.

There is
The pure music of forevermore
In the heart of becoming there
When the star-spangled
Banner waves across
Sea to shining sea.

How
The precipice of being
And nothingness looms

Overhead
As the desire for Truth
Mounts eons of time.

Then
The unknown opens
And vultures descend
Circling above and hungry.

Although
Self-deception
Rears its ugly head
I see through the window
Of time and space
To the beginning of life.

Opening my heart
To pure music
The phantom dances
Upon the reach of mind
And the stars and stripes
Forever marches
With what matters
Bringing Truth
As an awakening.

So
I am on a precipice
Paying for my lifestyle
Ass vultures follow me
Through time and space

But as I trance, I hear
The call of life resonating
In becoming there.

Then
I walk into pure music
Finding the way
The Truth and the life.

At the hour
Of final judgement
The old man sees
His time past
As a passage toward Truth
Although for stretches
He wavered
Oblivious of consequences.

Then
The mask of self-deception
Drops away and he counts
His transgressions.

He was known
To bare witness
To the way
The Truth and the life
As his destiny
As he, an artist

Painted the scene
Before the everlasting.

How
There were times
When demons raged
In his heart
And madness ruled
His actions.

So
There was evil
That took him
When he was mindless
And he knew
That he gave into it
Without a second thought.

Although
He poured out his heart
Asking for forgiveness
As the bells tolled Truth
He hoped that his faith
In The Word
Would speak for itself
Yet
He knew that his faith
Was not of his doing.

Then
He sits
Upon the mercy seat

Proclaiming his faith
In The Unknown God
As he weeps
Over his follies.

So
His time past is redeemed.

How great is forgiveness.

As time rolled into oblivion
And trance took becoming there
Into the center of things
In themselves
The phantom sang
Into the meat
Of the celestial clocks
And I awakened
To the moment.

There was
Magic in the air
That spirits drove
In patterns
Of red and black
And mind listened
To the drums of eternity.

Then
A crow sat

On a tombstone
While I walked
With the dead
As the graves tolled
Their story
And nothingness spoke
A language of mystery.

Reaching into thought
I felt the dynamic of life
Fill phenomenal reality
With possibility
As the phantom reduced
Time and space
Into the minute particular.

It did not matter
That Truth
Ran blindly into thought
As life escaped with the dead.

So
The ends of dasein collapsed.

So
A void spun wildly out of control.

So
My tranced took me
Into the deep touch.

Then
To conquer outliving self
Becoming there trumpeted
The spirit of the age
As the crow
Embraced the moment
With passion and conviction.

Looking down into the abyss
The phantom spied
The teeth of nothingness
As the blood of the ages
Swamped times and a half
As dasein slept
With the dead.

So
Despair ran ragged
Across the horizon
As times gave up
The living moment
While the patriot
Slept with the dead.

Then
The patriot opened
The now
To the rudiments

Of dasein
Finding them insufficient
For life.

It is
That dasein is
Destined to outliving self
With a hollow voice
Echoing destruction.

How
The scars of battle
Remind one
Of the horrors of war
And the look
Of the patriot reflects
The living dead.

Although the patriot
After tasting death
Marched into life
Burdened by his wounds
He knew
What it meant
To serve something
Greater than self.

Then
The phantom eased
The patriot into celebration
And he climbed
Out of himself

Into mission
Accomplished.

There is
The dream of life
Through mind
As the heart
Of duty wills
An awakening.

Because the phantom
Spoke to the wind
Through a portal
In cosmic consciousness
Becoming there inhaled
Whispers of Truth.

It was
The light
From the everlasting
That fed mind with images
Of celestial dynasties
As the principalities
Found pleasure in combat.

Although war
Tasted of death
And destruction
While peace sang

With sweet honey
It was that war is
Of the inevitable
Because of the darkness
In dasein's heart.

It was
The phantom that danced
With the rhythm
Defined by the moment
When to live and let live
Became pure music
But dasein did not listen
Scoffing at miracles.

Then
Time and spacer
Collided with what matters
And a crow launched mind
Beyond thought.

Then
Becoming there tranced
To another reality
Presided by the peace
Beyond understanding.

Then
Eternity became the moment
When possibility grew
Into life

And the phantom
Delivered the deep touch.

So
The agony of the ages
Poured
Into phenomenal reality
As becoming there
Trumpeted Truth.

In a wilderness of thought
Becoming there ventures through
The unknown
As dasein sinks
Into depravity.

It is not
That dasein is
But that it was
The past tense
In a language
Of self-deception.

To consummate the given
And then go further
Into the domain
Of cosmic consciousness
Becoming there uncovers
Hidden meaning

While dasein erects
A statue in its name
Proclaiming that it
Has arrived.

Blind to the substance
Of things in themselves
Dasein dwells
In the close at hand
As the celestial clocks
Strike a destiny
Of outliving-self.

How
Hollow the words of dasein.

How
Shallow the grave of dasein.

So
The close at hand
Begins the adventure
Into the unknown
As becoming there leaps
Into epiphany
Sung by the winds
Of a vertical column
Of time.

Then
Marking the milestones
Into the beyond

I trance
Into another reality
Where pure music
Defines the moment.

Then
The cosmic clock chimes
In my heart.

It was
The patriot who faced
The enemy out there
While in her heart
She knew her own demons.

So
She had demons
That taunted her
Confusing thoughts
O0f another kind
But the phantom helped her
Keep them in check.

Standing
Before a looking glass
She saw how duty
Drove her into battle
As the call of freedom
Infused her

With a right spirit
But there were moments
In quiet times
That she reflected
Upon her dreams
As she tranced
Into another reality.

Certainly
To be on the hunt
In the wilderness
Of back home
With her crosshairs
Targeted
On a twelve point buck
Proved to be
A distant dream.

Here
In the front lines
There was no time
For dreams
As she took fire
From a very real enemy.

Then
The phantom swooped down
Guarding the moment
As she shifted into survival
Yet
Ready to give her last breath
In the fight for freedom.

To be
In the rhythm
Of cosmic consciousness
How
The phantom brought her
To a safe place
Where the demons inside
And the enemy out there
Wasted away.

In the wilderness of mind
The biological clock
Flows to destiny
As becoming there
Searches for truth
As time empties
Dasein of substance.

There was
The power of cosmic
Consciousness
Nourishing becoming there
With the substance of life
While dasein withered
In the void
Of its own doing.

Then
The phantom, a trumpet

Announcing the moment
As victory
Opened phenomenal
Reality
To the way
The Truth and the life.

How
Faith in the Unknown God
Allowed becoming there
To prosper
While dasein consumed itself.

It is
That dasein has a god
Nothing other than self
And that belief strangles life
Until only dust remains.

How
Meditating on The Word
Delivers a vision
Of what matters
The signature of pure music
And becoming there
Witnesses
A celebration of Truth

So
The heart of Truth
Pounded eternity
Into the moment.

So
The phantom lives
In the reaches of the mind
Of becoming there.

So
Blessed assurance indwells
Through the biological clock.

With a crisp chill
Upon mind
Thought shifts
As the third eye
Penetrates
Time and times
And a half.

As becoming there
Thrown into phenomenal
Reality
Hunts for hidden meaning
The phantom uncovers
The mask of self
Deception.

Then
Cosmic consciousness
Transforms
The minute particular

Into the substance of life
As vultures gather
The bones
Of the living moment.

Then
The secrets
Of the living dead
Filter through the chill
And mind climbs
Out of itself.

There was
An army of the given
That marched into destiny
Their banner raised
Above smoke and fire.

There was
Truth in their steps
That braved
Across the sand
As the fallen
Never looked back.

How
The patriots followed
Their orders
As Truth flowed
Through their veins.

How
The trumpets sounded
Victory of life over death
As the spirit
Of the age fought
Against tyranny.

So
Freedom was their cause
As the third eye
Filled the moment
With Truth.

Peering
Into a crystal blue sky
I saw the phantom
Dancing into the unknown
As time and space
Echoed in my bones.

Then
Somewhere behind mind
A crow called to my heart.

It was
A joy of wonder
That took me
Into another reality
As I surveyed the expanse.

Drinking in
An elixir of cosmic
Consciousness
I staggered into trance
As thought took me
Into things-in-themselves
And a portal
To celestial dynasties
Opened in the sky.

Walking out of self
I joined hidden meaning
Exploring the substance
Of what matters
And visions formed
A melody of Truth.

It was
An epiphany of spirits
Trumpeting the moment
When becoming there grasped
The secrets known
To the beyond.

Then
The rub of life
Cast my third eye
Into the always already
There
And I circled
A wilderness of thought.

Then
The phantom took mind
Into a chasm
Of nothingness
And I saw the trace
Of self-deception.

Turning away
I leaped
Into the eternal light
Actualizing my deliverance
With the phantom
As becoming there
Rooted in Truth.

How
The deep touch
Brought us the breath
Of the everlasting.

Then
A vision stirred my heart
Feeling the rhythm
Of the cosmic clock
A time eternal.

It was
A space of grandeur
That eclipsed time

And times and a half
As pure music
Carried me far
Into possibility

So
A kingdom rose
In the sky
A glowing structure
That pulled me
Into the center
Of things-in-themselves
And I bent a knee
Before the throne
Of The Unknown God.

How
Great was the passage
Into the eternal.

Then
A crow flew down
Perching on my shoulder
And it placed
The spirit
Of the everlasting
Upon me.

I felt
The workings of The Word
Cosmic consciousness itself
And my mind read

The message
Between the words.

There was
Truth in becoming there
As I edged ever closer
To my destiny.

To be
In the presence
Of The Unknown God
Was to feel overpowered
By the muscle
Of forevermore
And I trembled
But it was a loving presence
Filled with life.

So
Through the trance
The deep touch
Cleared my vision
As my third eye
Wept with thankfulness.

To follow
The dance of the phantom
Her sway and flow
Across the expanse

How
Her face graced
Her presence
As her deep touch
Reached into my heart.

So
Her form celebrated
The living moment while I
Meditated
Upon her magic
And she carried my mind ubtio the center
Of phenomenal reality.

Then
She opened a portal
To the spirit
Of things-in-themselves
And the secrets
Of the beyond
Moved becoming there
Into pure music.

How
The image
Of celestial dynasties
Grew splendor before me
As the phantom
Took flight
In the form of a crow
And I rode

A parabola of time
To cosmic consciousness.

There is
A song that penetrates
The bones of the living
And its signature
Is one of beauty.

This song
Is the anthem
Of blessed assurance
As it moves my heart
Into the rhythm
Of the always
Already there.

What privilege it is
To be at the threshold
Breaking on the horizon
As time and space
Reveal the grace
Of her deep touch
And a crow
Takes me
Through a looking glass
To forevermore.

Time and times
And a half passed
As the old man centered
Himself upon trancing
And eternity opened
His way
To what matters.

It was not
That he deserved
Knowing the beyond
But it was given
To him
So that he could share
The light
Of the everlasting.

Although
He did not consider
Himself wise
He had been given
The authentic article
As his main stay.

So
The phantom took
The old man on high
And he trembled
Before the awesome might
Of this reality.

He saw
A house of many mansions
That encompassed
Becoming there
As he stood before
A fortress of wonder.

Breaking through the moment
Pure music elevates
His mind
To thoughts far beyond
The here and now
As the substance
Indwelling time and space
Configures his vision.

Then
Cosmic consciousness
Allows him to feel
Blessed assurance
As a crow leads him
Into things-in-themselves.

How
The splendor
Of The Unknown God
Infuses him with a right spirit
And he gives heartfelt thanks.

To witness
The origin of thought
The old man leaped
Into connectivity
From a platform
In juxtaposition.

So
One idea nested
Next to another
In liner time and space
Until a pattern surfaced
From one to another.

It was
An exercise
In trancing
From the here and now
To a reality beyond
All realities
A transcendence
Into the substance
Of becoming there.

Then
Mind throttles
Into the unknown
Passing one milestone
After another
Until the old man reaches
The deep touch.

Once he is there
The phantom takes
The moment
Stretching it
Into pure music
And the given
Feeds becoming there
With cosmic consciousness.

It all is
A leap of faith
Into endless possibility
As mind emanates
From the cutting edge
Of times and a half.

Then
The thing-in-itself
Surrounds the old man
With the substance
Of the close at hand
And becoming there
Pyramids
Into awesome wonder.

So
The origin of thought
Precipitates
From the always already there
As the phantom triggers
A vision through a leap
Of faith.

So
The origin of thought
Is pure music.

There is
A stand of trees
The ones in the foreground
Autumn like
But with the spirit
Of life
While those
Of the background
Seem as ghosts.

Vashakmadze painted it
That way
As a stirring moment
When the here and now
Entered the everlasting.

How
The trees entered
A deep sleep
As I climbed out
Of self and visions
Of another reality
Surfaced
From the unknown.

Then
My third eye followed
The shadows
Of times and a half
And the phantom
Placed hidden meaning
Into my heart.

Then
An armada of crows
Headed toward the horizon
As pure music moved me
Into the authentic article.

It is
A painting of mortality
When life walks
Into a wilderness
And the bite
Of self-deception
Devours dasein.

Mesmerized
By the light
Of becoming there
I gripped the moment
With the muscle
Of what matters
And the phantom
Allowed me
The freedom to be.

How
The stand of trees
Liberates thought
From the dull round
As the phantom issues
The deep touch.

Section 3
Liberty Of
Becoming There

In the garden
Of tables and chairs
Shadows of time past
Haunt the moment
As memories dart
Through the darkness.

Sinking into the abyss
Mind shuffles images
Of terror
And he cried out.

At one time
Madness scourged him
With visions of horror
As his blood turned
To a river of fire.

To live in despair
Feeling the ache of dread
He outlived himself
Because he wore
The mask of self-deception.

His life was a lie.

For a long time
Chaos tossed his bones
Into fits of anguish.

As he carried
The full weight
Of desolation
He thirsted for Truth
With the thought
That these times
Would pass.

There was
No relief until
What was there smashed
His teeth and pounded
His skull.

Then
He awoke to another reality
And the pain subsided.

It was
The phantom that took him

Into the breath
Of the living moment
And he found purpose
In a here and now
That led
To a peace beyond
Understanding.

How
The shadows of time past
Left scars
To be remembered
And to be endured.

As I go deeper
Into trance
The unknown registers
In mind
As hidden meaning.

There is no
Unknowable
Only the concealed.

What was once
Unknowable becomes
The concealed
As linear time issues
The light to vision.

So
Times and a half
Reveal the possible
Allowing the surfacing
Of the unknowable
And mind perceives
The inevitable
Through the looking glass
Of the trance.

Then
The magic
Of discernment
Occupies becoming there
And I see the way
The Truth and the life.

How
The third eye allows me
Into the reality
Of things-in-themselves
As I pyramid
Into the always
Already there.

Then
A crow massages thought
Until hidden meaning
Breaks through
To possibility
And the mystery
Of the beyond

Fills heart with promise.

Although
Cosmic consciousness
The workings
Of The Unknown God
Emanates Truth
Only
The deep touch reads
The writing on mind.

So
Through meditation
I enter the substance
Of being and nothingness
As the given
Takes me into a reality
Beyond phenomenal reality
The bedrock of the here
And now.

So
Is the table a table
Or an altar
Toi The Unknown God?

It is
The dawn of the everlasting
As the sun

Ventures from the unknown
And I climb out of self
To see hidden meaning.

A man stands
On a precipice
Overlooking the expanse
As the fog consumes
The here and now.

As a dark figure
He is the persona
Of the authentic article
As he listens
To the rhythm of eternity.

Close to the4 beginning
Of things in themselves
He calls my name
And mind eclipses dasein.

From beneath the fog
The world awakens
To mystery
And the wonder
Of becoming there.

So
Through the close at hand
One affirms self
The being and nothingness

Of what there is.

So
Proximity
To phenomenal reality
Establishes the ground
Of becoming there
As a point of departure
Into pure music.

How
The dawn of the everlasting
Allows the perception
Of another reality
One beyond the form
Of time and space
As the fog conceals substance
As becoming there grows
Into the authentic article.

Then
The phantom directed mind
Into beholding
The magic in and above
What is there.

So
He never has been
To Bagdad

Yet
He accepts that it
Is there.

So
He never has been
To Argentina
Yet
He accepts that it is there.

So
He never has been
To Peoria Illinois
Yet
He accepts that it
Is there.

The Truth of the matter
Is that he trusts
What he has learned
He believes
What he has been told.

How
Knowledge is grounded
In allowing assumption
To be trusted
As irrefutable given.

So
He does not believe
In God

Although he has heard
Of God.

It is
His life that has
Taught him
Not to trust those
Who speak of God
Because he has learned
To know better.

So
To him
The existence of God
Is the belief
In a virtual reality
A reality of fantasies
A reality of self-deception.

Although
One wanders
Through the close at hand
Mind builds a fortress
Of belief
Yet
Knowing nothing for sure.

Where
Assumption ends knowledge begins.

Where
Knowledge ends faith begins.

Where
Faith ends nothingness begins.

In the garden
Of tables and chairs
I sat with vultures
As the trumpet sounded.

It was
A time when life
Dissolved into nothingness
And despair filled
The moment.

So
The angels sat
At my side as I wept
Because it was
A day without light
Because dasein stole
The moment to be.

How
Time wasted in the shallows
Of thought
As mind fell into darkness.

How
In the inner parts

Of what matters
I fine no hope
And the dull round
Crushed my heart.

Then
Angels took me
Into a reality
Beyond realities
And I saw
Through a looking glass
The deep touch.

It became
A moment of triumph
When the center
Of all and everything
Shone brightly
And I felt trust
In The Word.

There is
That which is greater
Than self
A moment
When the vastness
Of the unknown smiles
Greeting the heart
With hope.

It is
In the presence

Of The Unknown God
That allows becoming there
To breathe the breath of life.

Suddenly
The sound of pure music
Addressed becoming there
As the old man struggled
Through time and space.

It was
The movement
Of the celestial clocks
That spoke rhythm
Into his bones
As he saw the eternal light
Across the horizon.

Then
A crow bolted
Out off no where
And the old man's
Biological clock
Shifted into trance.

It was
The suspension
Of all and everything
That took him

Into another reality
As he rode
A parabola of time
To forevermore.

Then
Through his third eye

The deep touch brought him
Into blessed assurance
And the crow fed him
A vision
Of things in themselves.

How
Mystery moves the earth
Of becoming there
Into an orbit
Of times and a half
As the dull round collapses
Before Truth.

So
The old man had struggled
His life a tragedy
Of blood and bone ache
Until he learned to trance.

Then
He realized that his life
Had worn the mask
Of self-deception.

Then
His life proceeded
Into pure music
Through The Word.

From far off
The echo of a crow
Stirred the light
Of what matters
As the third eye
Collected things
In themselves.

At first
There was a clutter of images
Each tantalizing
And then there were
The vast regions
Of nothingness.

To confront pure space
In the outer limits
Is to mirror possibility
As becoming there pushes self
Beyond dasein.

So
The substance of mind
And the rubric of thought

Takes the times
Of becoming there
Into pure music.

So
Possibility issues self
Into the domain of realities
And seeing the magnitude
Of the unknown
Feeds mind with the desire
To be.

How
Endless this possibility
As the weight of dasein
Buries mind
With the physics of darkness.

How
Vast is the view
Through the looking glass
As ideas grow into eternity.

Then
The phantom lights
On the beginning
Of time and space
As the celestial clocks
Number times and a half.

It is
The magic

Of pure music
That launches presence
Into the unknown.

So
The here and now is
The beginning
Of the always already there.

He was on a journey
To the center of mind
When being and nothingness
Upended phenomenal reality
And the fortress
Of ideation shot
Rockets into the beyond.

How
Traces to the unknown
Separated him from himself
As time thundered
Through the darkness.

Then
The phantom lit life
From beginning to end
As she wrote
Upon the muscle

Of becoming there
With flames of curiosity.

So
The hands
Of cosmic consciousness
Undressed reality with Truth
And the power
Of ideation traveled
Through the deep touch.

As he gathered
The fragments of mind
Into the table
Of what matters
The fortress of ideation
Became the dwelling place
Of his destiny
As he stepped
Inside himself.

There was
A trace to the other side
Of the unknown
Where the phantom drew
A passage out of darkness
To the light of pure music.

How
Wave upon wave pounded
Truth into form
And substance

As rockets exploded
Thought.

How
The countless realities
Numbered the dimensions
In tens of thousands.

Then
He found the beginning
Of the unknown
In the mathematics
Of becoming there
In the here and now.

Following the crow
Across the close at hand
Into the unknown
I inhaled the wonder
Of becoming there
As dasein drifted
Into oblivion.

Loosening the grip
Of dasein
The phantom allowed me
To advance into visions
Beyond the walls
Of self-deception.

The expanse of possibility
Liberated mind
From the trappings
Of the dull round
As the authentic article
Stirred my bones.

Then
The phantom bathed me
In pure music
As the deep touch
Infused me with Truth.

Suddenly
I was the movement
Upon a parabola of time
Looking into the interstices
Of mind
While the rhythm
Of eternity fed heart
With celestial dynasties.

Spiriting me away
From the darkness of dasein
The phantom launched me
Into the eternal light
Where life begins anew
And the crow danced
With becoming there.

Although I had been
Blind to Truth

The crow took my look
Transforming it
Into visions
Formed by the third eye.

I saw a crow
Above the signature of infinity
While times and a half
Calculated the here and now
With intelligent design.

To see
Into the awesome power
Of cosmic consciousness
Is to read the wonder
Of The Unknown God
As the biological clock
Climaxes in time and space.

So
The trance allowed me
To depart
From self-deception
And behold Truth.

As the bells tolled
The time of being
And nothingness
A chill fell

On the garden
Of tables and chairs.

Despair filled the air.

Casting a look
To the horizon
He formed the will
To be
Although life left
The living moment.

It was
A matter of digging
Himself out of a grave
While the dull round
Attacked sensibility
An age that buried Truth
As the principalities
Drew blood
From becoming there.

Seeing the rise of infamy
He equipped himself
With the will to endure
As shadows covered mind
With chaos.

Then
The phantom p[aced calm
In his heart
And peace in his mind

As she rebuked toe times.

It was
A moment when he saw the glory
Of The Unknown God
As this image held the power
Of all and everything.

Had he not suffered
He would not have known
Deliverance through The Word.

Then
In the garden
Of tables and chairs
Eternity trumpeted
Life onto forevermore.

When the old man
Looked into the mirror
He saw a mountain
Crumbling into the sea
And he turned to the phantom
For the signature
Of life.

She set his desire
On fire as he leaped
Into becoming there.

It was
A mixture
Of the authentic article
And pure music
That stormed
Through the moment
As he chose to be.

He saw
How there was
Being rather than
Nothingness
And the phantom pulled
The trigger on despair.

Pyramiding out of self
He reached for Truth
Gaining a vision
Of the always
Already there.

It is
That life is a promise
And death is a given.

Although
The age fed upon deceit
There was a way
Out of self-deception
Founded upon trusting
The Unknown God.

So
The phantom taught him
The way to Truth
And life
By meditating on The Word
And he leaned on his vision
Of forevermore.

He was not
Afraid of death
Because of his blessed
Assurance
And he did not fear life
Because he dwelled
With pure music.

So
The old man conquered
The dull round
By his will to be
By his faith
In the Unknown God
As his thoughts
Configured the substance
Of the close at hand
Into pure music.

It was
That he throttled

Through time and space
With the promise
Of life in his breath
As becoming there
Fractured self-deception.

He lived
With the authentic article
In his heart
As he passed
Through the here and now
Onto forevermore.

The taste
Of what matters
Fueled his presence
To probe possibility
Penetrating
Into the unknown
With the deep touch.

It was his
To decipher the language
Of hidden meaning
Affixing the mystery
Of life
With the vision of the beyond
But it was
The will of his spirit
That allowed him
To endure.

Although
Tragedy struck the old man
Again and again
He saw his way
Through the debris
Of dasein
With unwavering hope.

He trusted himself
Which allowed him to trust
The given
As he scaled the walls
Of infamy.

It was
The symmetry
Of his presence
That persevered
Through nothingness.

It was
His will to be
And his faith
In The Unknown God
That allowed him
To read hidden meaning.

He is destined
To document

The way of Truth
As he collected
The dots and dashes
Leading to the beyond.

At the threshold
Of the abyss
He pictured the point
Of no return
And then looked
Oblivion in the eye.

Knowing the phantom
Led him
Into the mystery
Of becoming there
As he beheld
Pure music
Through a portal
In a parabola of time.

So
Through the abyss
He learned
The length and breadth
Of self-deception
As time and space
Defined the limitations
Of dasein
As a looking glass
Revealed the freedom
Of becoming there.

Because he reached
The authentic article
Through the archeology
Of Truth
His heart fed on The Word.

He gathered
From his walk
Upon a parabola of time
The language
Of nothingness
Because he felt
The depth of despair.

So
He found forevermore
In the here and now.

Sitting on the edge
Of time and space
He bled thought
Into the moment.

It was
In the garden
Of tables and chairs
That he explored
The source of ideation

As time passed
Mind grew into curiosity
As a rain flushed
The air clean.

He drew an image
In the circle
Of becoming there
Tapping into cosmic
Consciousness.

Through trance
He saw a shining sphere
That danced to the rhythm
Of pure music
As angels hovered
On high.

Where there was darkness
A light shone
Bringing an infusion
Of wonder
As mind entered
A two-dimensional reality.

Then
As an archeology
Of presence
He excavated being
And nothingness.

Time severed
From times and a half
And he willed himself
Through milestones
Of realities.

It was
That the source
Of ideation
Was the relationship
Between juxtaposition
Connectivity and a leap
Of faith.

So
First there were elements
Followed by the connection
Of forms
That resulted
In a leap of faith
The emanation
Of an idea.

What defined each
Of these milestones
Was energy
With the source
In cosmic consciousness.

Then
Angels trumpeted
The appearance of Truth

The pure music
Of all and everything.

So
He wondered
Which was greater
All and everything
Or the universe.

The grey clouds
Enveloping the sky
Concealed the everlasting
Although there was
The promise
Of becoming there.

It was not
That he was
A static presence
Not dasein
But that he was
A movement
From phenomenal reality
To pure music
As the mathematics
Of time and space
Calculated endless
Possibility.

It was
That he reached
For cosmic consciousness
As an endeavor
From his heart
Finding Truth
In the expanse.

Opening
His third eye
To the presence
Of the eternal light
He found beauty
In the always already there
The close at hand
And the substance
Of mind.

He found eternity
In a grain of sand
In the fearful symmetry
Of what was there.

Although the clouds
Enveloped the sky
He moved from feelings
To thoughts
As the celestial clocks
Spoke with the voice
Of forevermore.

Although the clouds
Enveloped the sky
He rode a parabola of time
Into destiny
An overture
To what matters.

So
He read the hidden meaning
In the dull round
Eclipsing the debris
Of the linear
Approaching the wonder
Of The Unknown God.

As the mountain ridges
Hide in the fog
I step outside myself
To visit the eternal.

There is
An awakening of the bones
And a quickness to mind
That advances
Into the unknown.

Among the traces
To what is there
The sound of pure music

Purges the heart
As I seek
Hidden meaning
In the expanse.

Intertwined
In the fog are the bells
That signal the beginning
Of a moment
When the third eye
Penetrates timelessness.

Then
The who that I was
Ignites time and space
With magic
Found in dasein.

It was
That the third eye
Envisioned the concealed
As one reality
After another
And I raised the voice
Of life from the rubble
Of the dull round.

Then
I passed
Into the language
Of the here and now
To pull becoming there

Into what matters
And trumpets let loose
A trembling in the heart.

I was walking through the fog
While the third eye
Eclipsed being and nothingness.

I was there and not there.

So
The shadows of infamy
Straddle the moment
And time stands still.

To dwell in darkness
Bleeds the living of life
As hiding behind
A mask of deceit
Leads to self-deception.

There is
An encompassing despair
To the wits of dasein
As the mountains
Bury the living and the dead.

To look
In the mirror

Of what is there
Seeing nothingness
Allows suffering to flourish
In the interstices of mind.

How
Empty the thoughts
Of darkness.

However
To explore the other side
Of time and space
Awakens moments of Truth
The light of the always
Already there.

There is
No darkness
In pure music
As it delivers the heart
To the everlasting
As the deep touch
Carries mind into splendor.

Then
Surrounded by light
Becoming there sees Truth
In the substance
Of times and a half
As the reality of realities
Issues life
Onto forevermore.

So
It is a matter
Of choosing darkness
Or be chosen
By the light of The Word.

Within the still wasters
Of time and times
And a half
I seek the strength
To carry on
While the urge
To abandon life
Staggers the mind.

How
When facing the void
The heart labors
And mind struggles
From thought to thought.

The bones weary
As they are
Carry the form
Of becoming there
Into the substance
Of the close at hand
And I see hope
In a moment to be.

So
There is an awakening
And I feel
The light of eternity
Infuse within me
The life
Of what matters.

So
When enervation persists
Life insists.

Then
The power of cosmic
Consciousness
Opens my heart
To the living moment
And a world of possibility
Envelopes time and space.

To be
Along the ride
To eternity
With purpose in the heart
How
The Word offers
The strength to carry on.

It is
The void
With the devastation
Of the abyss

That steals the breath
Of life
But the power
Of The Unknown God
Takes the self
Into the reality
Of pure music.

As the earth turned
Into a world of possibility
He pursued hidden meaning
Through the trance.

To allow mind
Access to eternity
How
A parabola of time
Serves as the portal
To the deep touch
And becoming there
Witnesses the feel
Of the anatomy of time
And space.

Because
The third eye penetrates
The mask of dasein
Beholding the feel
Of self-deception

Thought follows
The trace to Truth
Far into the unknown.

Milestone after milestone
Passes into oblivion
As the child of him
Launches ideation
Into the moment.

To be buried in thought
Is to liberate the substance
Of the close at hand
As his spirit unearths
The existential moment.

Then
He answered the call
Of Truth
And his heart
Throbbed
With what matters.

So
It is curiosity
That dug his way
Through possibility
Onto the essence
Appearing
In the looking glass
And he built and altar there
To The Unknown God.

How
Times and a half
Brought him
Into the presence
Of eternal light
As he bent a knee
Before The Word.

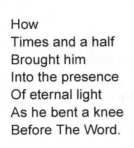

So
It is that curiosity
Emanates from the child
In him
As all and everything
Exists
In posasibility.

As the field
Of the encompassing
Opens through
T
The looking glass
The adult discerns
The substance
Of what is there
As mind feels
The proximity
Of hidden meaning.

Then
Energy charges thought
Into the becoming there
And the unknown
Appears as the given.

To launch
From the always
Already there
Into becoming there
The parent grasps
The hidden meaning
Within phenomenal reality
With curiosity
As the need to be.

So
The crux of becoming there
Is through the three
Personas within him.

How
Language forms
All and everything
Into an equation
Of metaphors
With the enlightenment
Of nothingness
As part of the given.

So
Even nothingness exists

In the realm of possibility
But more of a function
Of language
Than phenomenal reality.

If
Being is a given
To the parent within him
Then nothingness
Is a given
In the unknown
Waiting for curiosity
To unearth its existence

So
Nothingness exists
As a feeling
Devoid of being
The negation
Of curiosity
The subtext of oblivion.

Where oblivion is
Nothingness exists.

In endless possibility
All and everything exists
According
To the cosmic clock

But what is probable
Becomes more of a myth
Based on the limitations
Of linear time and space.

So
He calculates possibility
With the rubric
Of the known
As a given
Extending the here and now
Into proximity
While he measures
The gravity of darkness.

Then
The bells chime
The crows take flight
And the rudiments
Of existential thought
Weigh the substance
Of becoming there.

How
Mind voids an equation
Of time and times
And a half
Employing the calculus
Of nothingness
With imaginary numbers
As the feeling
Of epiphany launches him

Out of a sea of sweat
Onto the next horizon.

Once there
He figures illusion
Into fact
As his formula proves
That he existed.

So
His formula testifies
That there are
Only three dimensions
Under the governance
Of the cosmic clock
While he sketches
His biological clock
Into the moment.

So
The moment
Takes the form
Of the during
That stretches
Toward cosmic consciousness.

Calculating the domain
Of nothingness
He ascribes imaginary numbers

Concluding that nothingness
Is a negative coefficient
A negative one.

So
The square root
Of a negative sixty-four
Is minus one times eight.

Then
He saw
In the looking glass
The mystery of gravity
And how it was
A function
Of dark energy
The subtext
Of nothingness.

Laughing at himself
He saw how mind
Could fabricate probability
From the unknown
Stretching possibility
Into thingness.

How
Foolish a mind
That thinks its way
Into the abyss
While Truth tugs
At his heart.

So
Curiosity feeds
The moment
When he leaps out of himself
Exploring the wonder
That dwells in the substance
Of thee close at hand.

Thus
He concludes
That the mechanism
Of gravity is levity
As time reverses itself
Through the big laugh.

To understand
All and everything
Is the driving force
Behind his will to be
As his laughter
Carries him
Beyond phenomenal reality.

So
He is the thing in itself
And imaginary numbers define
The parallel universe.

SECTION 4
AN EMPTY MIND

To endure
To fight back
The tide of outliving self
The phantom taught him
The ways of becoming there
As he faced the abyss.

To have
An insatiable appetite
For Truth
Led him to another
Horizon of life
Where purpose filled
Times and a half.

He knew
That as long as there was
The unknown
He would find purpose

With the pursuit of Truth
As his driving engine.

Of course
There was the additional
Power of exploring beauty
But the greatest
Incentive
Was serving
The Unknown God.

Although
There were times
When he wavered
From his faith
He always returned
To The Word.

Looking back, he could see
How The Word carried him
Through the abyss
Empowering becoming there
With the stamina
To endure
As he returned to faith.

So
It was a gift
To overcome dread
That was his life
And it was the phantom

Who loved him more
Than he loved himself.

How
The pursuit of Truth and beauty
Infused his third eye
With the vision of possibility
Beyond where he was.

Then
He turned to the way
Of Truth and life
And the promise
Of becoming there.

Through nothingness
The cold grips the bones
And I submerse myself
In the deep touch.

Here
In the meadow of mind
Blooms eternity
And the thunder
Of the existential moment
Derives the essence
Of times and a half
As my thoughts connect
To a harvest of feelings.

To live at the edge
Where the crow speaks
Of freedom
How
Pure music delivers me
Advancing what I am
Into the celebration
Of blessed assurance.

So
There is Truth in the heart
That answers
The call of the crow
And I rise above thought.

Penetrating the unknown
I follow The Word
Into the everlasting
As the crow signals
The advent of the deep touch.

Then
The cold covers my breath
With the light
Of becoming there
And I embrace the phantom.

She is
The heart of time and space
That warms thee blood of life.

She is
The crow and the life
Of the crow
As I drink in the moment
And the cold warms
In the light
Of cosmic consciousness.

So
Through the looking glass
Of the phantom
Understanding grows
Exponentially.

Struggling
Through time and space
Surrounded by nothingness
He stepped into the moment
And all and everything
Exploded with splendor
Because he found there
The phantom.

Radiant
As she was
He thought of time
And times and a half
When his heart
Wooed her

When his mind prospered
In her light.

It was
In the now
That she traced
Hidden meaning
Into his heart
As he followed the crows
To forevermore.

While in trance
He suspended time
To see through
The looking glass
To the other side
Of the here and now
As trumpets proclaimed
The glory
Of The Unknown God.

Entering
A parabola of time
Brought him ever closer
To cosmic consciousness
As his thoughts
Leaped into the unknown.

Then
The phantom took him
Into the center
Of things in themselves

Leading him
Into an understanding
Of what matters most.

It was
His faith that carried him
Into pure music
As the phantom
Poured the authentic
Article
Into his being.

Then
He undressed her kiss.

Then
The crow spoke
A wilderness into mind
And I saw through tranced
A land of milk and honey.

There was
Peace in the moment
And brotherhood in the blood
As cosmic consciousness
Took me far into the beyond.

Then
The crow set a fire

In the sky
And the flames
Bathed the earth in Truth.

Encompassing
The moment
Pure music brought me
Into tender regions
Of time and space
Stirring the authentic
Article
Into becoming there.

Standing tall
The mystery tree
Brought life
To the breath
Of hidden meaning
As the phantom
Danced in my heart
And understanding
Allowed me to witness
An age of splendor.

How
Eternity took this moment
Into the unknown
Leaving times and a half
And the celestial clocks
Drew a silhouette
Of forevermore
Into a looking glass

As I knelt before the altar
To The Unknown God.

There was
An epiphany
To the moment
As trance traced the steps
To always and forever
And I lifted my life
Into service to The Word
Because of the calling.

So
The land of milk and honey
Dwells in the heart
Of becoming there.

To bask in the light
Of The Unknown God
I find Truth
Through becoming there.

Then
Eternity opens the moment
When time and space
Delivers me
To blessed assurance
And the mask
That was me disappears.

Trumpeting The Word
Across being and nothingness
I land in a garden
Of promise
As the authentic article
Speaks from my heart.

So
Belief is a step
Out of self
And into what matters.

So
Truth is a matter
Not of thought or feeling
Bus a leap of faith.

Although
Time and times and a half
Cloud the vision
Of forevermore
It is the light
Of The Word
That builds a kingdom
Of splendor in the heart.

As the celestial clocks
Ease time into space
I reach through a portal
And embrace the unknown.

How
Nothingness empties thought
Of life
As the given determines
The passion
That drives self
Either into the abyss
Or the epiphany
Of the deep touch.

So
Truth dwells
In the beyond
And through the deep touch
Visits self.

So
One either chooses
Nothingness
Or is chosen by Truth.

Then
Through trance
I see the phantom
In all her beauty
As she visits me
In the garden
Of tables and chairs.

She is
A persona of splendor
Flourishing in my heart
Taking thought
Into the mysteries
Of the unknown.

She is
The passageway
 Into immaculate dreams
The portal to promise
As she drums Truth
Into becoming there
And I view her
As the signature
Of pure music.

She is
The persona of the dance
That eternity thinks
Into a moment.

How
The thing in itself
Trembles
Through time and space
As the phantom
Excavates nothingness
Issuing the advance
Into the always already
There.

It is
The experiential
That dictates to dasein
As an outmoded design
An echo on agony
And the folly
Of a dead age.

Suddenly
The phantom awakens
Truth
In the body
Of what is there
And the garden
Of tables and chairs
Explodes in ecstasy.

It is here
That she warms the mind
With the deep touch
And Truth writes the will
To be.

She is strong, powerful
And she weighs
All and everything
In her hands
Carrying the load
Of eternity on her back.

She is the image
Of the always already there
As time shifts to a moment
As space cries out
Affirming her presence .

To be
The persona
Of the everlasting
Is far beyond
Time and space
Yet
She is true to the spirit
Of the authentic article
And lives in the bones
Of the here and now.

As the celestial clocks
Chime
She rises from the earth
Of what matters
And times and a half
Birth nothingness
Into being.

How the mask
Of dasein
Disintegrates
Before her face
As she dances
Into the unknown.

Then
She lays her spirit
Upon my heart
And I feel the rub
Of life
As Truth towers
In my mind.

It is
An edifice
Of a vertical
Column of time
That she constructs
And I enter that unknown
With passion.

To cherish her
Is to know
The deep touch
Of the phantom.

She is the one who led me
To The Unknown God.

In the quiet
Of a slow rain
Nothingness speaks
Of the unknown
And I carry thoughts

Into the looking glass
Of time and space
Toward unsettling mysteries.

How
To stretch the vision
From the close at handed
To horizons beyond thought
Allows me to explore
Hidden meaning
As I behold the thing
In itself
The essence
Of becoming there.

It is
The living moment
A breath away
From the here and now
That liberates the spirit
From times and a half
And the unknown
Takes flight
With the crows.

Then
From the quiet
Of a slow rain
Truth heads my way
And the image
Of what is there

Unfolds the light
Of cosmic consciousness.

So
Before there was
Nothingness
There is the always
Already there
The promise
Of the everlasting.

So
Pure music is
The movement
From here to the beyond
As the now emerges
In eternity.

How
The unsettling mysteries
Yield to the vision
Through the looking glass
And the rush
Of a trumpet summons mind
Toward cosmic consciousness.

To know eternity
What treasure
Is this blessed assurance.

When is
Enough, enough
As he loaded his mind
With howitzers.

There is
The trace to hidden meaning
In the ramparts
Of being and nothingness
As he arms his being
With the bayonet
From celestial clocks
And the walls
Of self-deception crumble.

He yearned
For the full body
Of the everlasting
Finding it in the way
Of Truth and life
As he shot his way
Out of darkness
And into the light
Of forevermore.

Inside his mind dwells
The authentic article.

Inside his heart dwells
Blessed assurance.

Then
He drinks in
The courage of ages
And affixes his sights
On folly and ignorance.

To be
With the vibrations
Of pure music
He follows the trumpet
Of battle
Launching his mind
Into the unknown.

To unearth
The bunkers of ignominy
He explodes thoughts
Gathered by following
The traces toward
A vertical column of time.

Then
Approaching callous regions
Of hidden meaning
He is equipped
With an inkling
Of cosmic consciousness
As he marches into hell fire.

He is
A soldier, a patriot

And the artist
Of always and forever.

There is
Nothing common
About common folk
As the heart hears
The song of liberty.

They are
The backbone of a nation
Spiriting life
With the work of their hands
As the sun rises
As the sun sets.

Living day by day
They capture the essence
Of what matters.

It is not
Power that they
Are after
Not fortune or fame
But the sustenance
For carrying on
Providing for family.

They are
The very center
Of what humanity
Is about
And they cherish
What money can't buy.

Their hope
Is in their children
And the generations to come
As the world
Spins with madness.

How
Eternity knows them
By name and their faces
Document the walls
Of forevermore.

They don't
Believe in magic
Or an order of the fancy
But they adhere
To the laws
That humanity
Has always known.

To live, to carry on
To provide
For their needs
They cherish their freedom
And grow meaning into life.

Transcending time and space
I see
A golden house
Of many mansions
Glowing in the quickened light
Of the always already there
And a rhapsody
From celestial dynasties
Liberates dasein
Onto the presence
Of becoming there.

There is no
Bondage in this moment
Because the unchained force
Of cosmic consciousness
Sees me through
The vast regions
Of nothingness.

Then
I lift my third eye
To a gathering look
Into eternity
As The Word speaks
Times and a half
Across the travels
Of becoming there.

So
The moment explodes
With wonder.

So
This sense of presence
Expands onto the threshold
Of the everlasting
As The Unknown God
Shows me my destiny
Through a parabola of time.

Reaching
The palm at the end
Of thought
I feel an epiphany
Rise from my blood
As my heart finds
Blessed assurance
And my triumph
Over self-deception
Rockets across the universe.

There is
Certainty in the heart
And conviction in mind
That transcends dasein
And I climb out of self
To fathom the way
To Truth and life.

How
This trance allows me
To visit the kingdom
Of The Unknown God
The always already there
From the here and now.

There is
A mystery harbored
In the heart of the crow
And it carries
The rhythm of life
Itself.

It is
A higher order of things
With shades of trust
Reaching to the whole
Spectrum of Truth.

Where Truth is in colors
Trust is in shades of gray.so
Trust is the shadow
Of Truth
As mind grapples
With existential thingness
While Truth
Is the light beyond
Thingness

As seen through
The third eye.

How
The spirit
Of the crow brings light
To becoming there
And the colors of Truth
Summon pure music
Into the blood
Of what is there.

So
Cosmic consciousness
Speaks radiant colors
Into becoming there
And the crow
Infuses them into mind.

To see
Through the looking glass
Of the close at hand
Allows Truth
To resonate thought
Into an epiphany
And becoming there
Trusts its light.

So
From the heart
Of the crow pours
This mystery

Onto times and a half
As hidden meaning
As Truth incarnate
Flourishes through trance.

Walking into the unknown
Undressing hidden meaning
I pyramid
Through time and space
Riding the ridges
Of a two-dimensional
Reality.

With the third eye
I gather the circles
Of vultures
As they design
The beginning and end
Of what is there.

In this cemetery
Spirits rise, speaking
Truth into the wind.

Climbing
Onto the other side
Of being and time
I feel the deep touch
Of the everlasting

As the celestial clocks
Chime the hour
When vultures feed
On the moment.

Here
In this graveyard
Thoughts wrestle
With the no longer
While becoming there
Pursues the way of Truth.

There is
A trembling of the earth
When the phantom pours
Pure music into the heart
And the thinking
Of what matters most
Discharges self-deception.

From a parabola of time
I leap into visions
Of the always already there
In tune with the cosmic clock.

Then
I see Golgotha of long ago
And I weep.

So
I dig myself
Out of the grave

Of thought
And walk
With the phantom
To forevermore.

Then
We follow the wind of Truth
On wings of hope and faith.

To face the abyss
Gathering hidden meaning
I enter another reality
Where the phantom
Suspends time.

It is
A moment
Extending far beyond
Nothingness
And the image
Of The Word
Welcomes me.

Amazed
Becoming there spins
Into a thin mist
And the third eye focuses
Upon the light
Of always and forever.

Then
A crow opens the expanse
To the splendor
Of the living moment
When the passage
To the deep touch
Of The Unknown God
Encompasses
Time and space.

Suddenly
The crow feeds the moment
With life
And spirits rise
Through the drift
Of things in themselves.

It is
That Truth draws
The breath
Of pure music
And a rhapsody
Issues the mystery
Of blessed assurance.

So
I think myself
Into the authentic article
As the phantom embraces
The beyond
And the darkness
Of the abyss turns

To the light
Of understanding.

Then
The phantom spreads
Her wings
Across the abyss
As hidden meaning yields
To the deep touch
And becoming there
Awakens to Truth.

Through trancing
I have seen the phantom
In all her splendor
And I felt
The rise of eternity
In visions of pure music.

Her radiance transcends
The here and now
As she approaches
Through the darkness
Before dawn.

How
Truth speaks to the heart
With concepts
From the deep touch

And I open my mind
To the message
From the phantom.

At the eve
Of time and space
She configured a crown
Of glory
Across the expanse
As I purge myself
Of self-deception.

In her look
Is a universe of wonder
And she graces the moment
With stellar secrets.

So
Feelings start the connection
To inner space
And mind deciphers
The rhythm of the beyond
Until the moment
Coalesces into epiphany.

How
The words of the phantom
Liberate becoming there
From the cages
Of hidden meaning.

How
Her voiced penetrates
The long silence of dasein
As I lift
My third eye
Into a look of the always
Already there.

Then
From the looking glass
Of forevermore
She takes my heart
Into the wilds of passion
And I breathe again
The breath
Of the living moment.

So
The spirit was with me
While I walked through the wilds.

Time and times
And a half passed
And the wilderness
In all its beauty
Filled my heart
With purpose.

When I came
To a river
Visions stirred the moment
And I felt blessed assurance.

It was
A moment of Truth
In abundance
That flooded my mind
With the authentic article
As I stepped out of self
To find becoming there.

I had seen
Aa river of hope
A sensation that rubbed
Passion into my heart
And I trusted
The visions of forevermore.

Then
I teleported to the garden
Of tables and chairs
And the spirit followed me.

Legions of angels
Numbering in the thousands
Trumpeted the glory
O0f The Unknown God
And I witnessed
Why there was being
Rather than nothingness.

Spiraling through trance
I heard the voice
Of pure music
As the presence
Of what mattered most.

It is
That the garden
Of tables and chairs
Is the outpost
Where the deep touch
Emanates from the beyond
And into becoming there.

As the moment
Charges with the engine
Of the always already there
Cosmic consciousness
Infuses the living
With veritable life.

So
The phantom is
From the other side
Of phenomenal reality
A place of mystery
And she uncovers
All hidden meaning.

With her talents
She rubs passion
Into becoming there
And I sigh with relief.

Seeking her paradigm
Of darkness and light
I follow her traces
To the beyond
As time and space
Become a two-dimensional
Reality.

Suspended
In the looking glass
I feel her deep touch
As my substance
Explodes in ecstasy.

This is
A moment when times
And a half stretch mind
Into an array of colors
And the authentic article
Takes me
Into pure music
An epiphany
Of the everlasting.

Then
The phantom releases
A charge of dynamics

That opens the third eye
To the unknown
As I step further
Into trance.

Here
The drums of eternity
Summon life
Into my bones
And the heart
Of what matters
Drives me far
Into the unknown.

How
The mystery of this moment
Carries thought
Into the image that she is
As she grips
My meat with desire.

So
The phantom takes me
Into the garden
Of tables and chairs
Where she trumpets me
Into a pyramid
Of forevermore
The deep touch
Of cosmic consciousness.

SECTION 5
WITH SPIRITS OF LIFE

To explore the interstices
Of time and space
As simply a presence
Allows becoming there
To navigate through the unknown
Milestone by milestone.

In the heavens
There is a light
With the rise of dawn
And darkness fades
By the will
Of cosmic consciousness.

It is
To yield to the power
Of The Unknown God
Is to venture
Into the deep touch

Filled with the spirit
Of what matters.

Where light reaches shadow
The moment springs
Into a parabola of time
As I rise
With the blood of eternity.

There is
The calling of the celestial
Clocks
That displays hidden meaning
And the phantom opens
My third eye to The Word.

Then
I pass over the abyss
That separates the now
From forevermore
And the phantom dances
Across creation
Bringing me ever closer
To pure music.

To breathe in
The breath of life
Transforms dasein
Into becoming there
And I leave self-deception
To the mask
Of the dull round.

Then
The phantom forms
Destiny by the geometry
Of the celestial clocks
And I milk Truth
From the authentic article.

So
Blessed assurance
And the authentic article
Are parallel concepts.

Equipped with purpose
He blasted
Through time and space
Exploring the unknown
With a powerful drive
With an engine
Of the deep touch.

He rode
With the phantom
Through life
On a never ending road
Of fulfillment.

He followed the sun.

He followed the stars.

As the road led
Across the horizon
And into the everlasting
The phantom gave3 him
The sweet sweat
Of the authentic article
And he rode with promise
In his heart.

He finally lived
In good days
Leaving outliving himself
Far behind.

Although
There were times
When he struggled
When demons bent his mind
He found that
All that
Was the price he had to pay
To gain his faith
In The Word.

So
He hit the road
With the phantom
Tearing down to what mattered
As his heart followed
The rhythm
Of the cosmic clock.

It was
Eternity that he headed for
As the miles
Into the unknown passed
As a celebration
Of becoming there.

So
Through the ride
He found blessed assurance
A jubilation onto forevermore
And the phantom
His true love
Smiled.

Then
Out of the wilds
A crow called
Stirring my mind
With a rhapsody
Of pure music.

It was
A beauteous movement
Spiraling through time
And times and a half
As my trance fostered
Images of blessed angels.

It was
A litany of treasures
From the beyond
That radiated Truth
Into becoming there
As the phantom
Embraced me
With the deep touch.

How
The moment suspended
Thought as my heart
Felt a beacon
Of eternal light
As the phantom
Showed me
The trace
To hidden meaning.

Seeing
The phantom in all
Her splendor
I entered the looking glass
Of the always already there
And trumpets sounded.

Then
There was silence.
Then the bells of forevermore
Chimed.

Then
The gates of eternity opened
And the phantom
Pulled me to the other side.

How
The trance took me
Into the far reaches
Of the unknown
Here possibility is born
As my heart grew
Into what mattered.

I felt
The triumph
That only
The authentic article
Could bring.

To live
No longer with the mask
Of self-0deception
I found the peace
Beyond understanding
In my blessed assurance.

In the garden
Of tables and chairs
Becoming there prospers

In the understanding
Of mysteries
Because he explores
The unknown
To reveal hidden meaning.

Through the trance
He uncovers
The always already there
Within things
In themselves.

It is
The destiny of becoming there
To reach into the substance
Of what matters
Gathering the realities
Of the authentic article
As he drinks in
Moments of Truth.

While in trance
He pulls out
The domain of possibility
As the vast horizons
Of times and a half
Unfold into a parabola
Of time.

To leave
Linear time allows
Becoming there

To tap into the celestial
Clocks
As the trance opens
A portal to the beyond.

Through the workings
Of meditation
He lets loose the power
Of pure music
And the masks
Of the close at hand
Drop away.

So
It is taking the vision
Of the always already there
Into the grasp
Of the deep touch
That allows traces
To the subtexts of life
Ands the heart reads
Figures behind the shadows
On the cave wall.

Then
The secrets of eternity
Take becoming there
Into the dance
Of pure music.

So
There is a reason

Why there are only
Three dimensions.

Tuning
Into the deep touch
Through trance
I feel the presence
Of The Unknown God
As the phantom rubs life
Into becoming there.

There is
The movement of mind
Into the dawn of possibility
As she pulls me
Into another reality
And visions fill
My third eye.

Then
The scarlet sky blooms radiant
As red wine flows
From the sun.

Then
The earth rises
As leaven bread
And the phantom

Takes becoming there
Into a parabola of time.

From there
I see linear time spin
Into the always
Already there
As she infuses me
With the breath
Of cosmic consciousness.

As she wove becoming there
In and out
Of phenomenal reality
I launched into the expanse.

Then
The drums of eternity
Pound life into my heart
And my mind fathomed
The beat of the everlasting.

Then
My passion for Truth
Filled me
With the peace
Beyond understanding
And the celestial clocks
Revealed hidden meaning
As the picture of forevermore.

It was
To be as the wind blows
As the waves of the sea
Find the shore
As pure music fills mind
With the deep touch.

Here is The Unknown God.

Here I am.

To know the way, the Truth
And the life
Is to transcend the dull round
Entering the domain
Of cosmic consciousness.

It is
A calling to thee heart
That allows the third eye
To receive the presence
Of The Unknown God.

Then
Pure music embraces
Becoming there
With the light
Of the everlasting
And the phantom

Kicks away the mask
Of self-deception.

Hungering
For the mysteries
Within the close at hand
An old man deciphers
The subtexts
Of becoming there
Revealing why there is
Being rather
Than nothingness.

In the moments
Beyond the here and now
An epiphany carries him
Into what matters
As a crow signals
The beginning
Of forevermore.

Then
Bells chime the hour
When time and space
Follow the celestial clocks
And he sees the coming
Of the peace
That transcends
Time and space
An understanding
Of existential hopes

And dreams
And all that matters.

So
The concept of becoming there
Erases dasein
As the dance of the phantom
Configures a reality
Of possibility
And the old man listens
To the crow's heart
As it forms the subtext
Of the always already there.

So
The old man visited
The always already there
With his third eye
That saw
Things in themselves
As a myriad of possibility.

To discern
What was there
From what was Truth
Allowed him to see
In the looking glass
Visions of the everlasting.

It was
A matter of dropping
The mask of self-deception
And allowing
Cosmic consciousness
To feed ideation.

In becoming there
He learned the passage
Through the beyond
Onto a wilderness of being.

There
He found life
Beyond linear time

It w
That he was chosen
To grasp the weight
Of the existential moment
As he turned to the phantom
For the scale of Truth.

In her substance
She formed pure music
As the trumpets
Celebrated becoming there
And the drums of eternity
Drove Truth
Into his destiny.

Then
From the garden
Of tables and chairs
He followed the crow
Into the death of dasein
And becoming there
Believed itself
Into what matters.

It was
That the old man found
The deep touch by tapping
Into cosmic consciousness
And Truth flowed
In his blood.

Through trance he fathomed
Juxtaposition and connectivity
To a leap of faith.

So
The old man, Truth
And cosmic consciousness
Are one.

Into the heart
Of phenomenal reality
Where substance precedes form
The old man pushes

The limits of being
And nothingness
As the phantom feeds
Him possibility.

This is
An existential moment
When becoming there cries out
From bones
Raw with misgivings
And the old man
Bows his head in prayer.

Although
He thought himself
Serving
The Unknown God
As he looked
Into his life with trembling
He feared the validity
Of his endeavors.

He thought
That he was chosen
To witness the grace
Of The Word.

Then
He opened his third eye
To the Truth
Humbled before the throne
Of the everlasting.

As he projected himself
Through meditation
His heart lived
With blessed assurance
But his mind found
Him lost.

Then
He leaped into the unknown
With passion and hope
As he yearned
For the peace beyond
Understanding.

Finding himself
Beyond time and space
He knew that he was lost
Without The Unknown God.

Then
The phantom embraced him
With the way
The Truth and the life
And he shook hands
With his faith.

Although
There are moments
When mind spins in doubt
The power of cosmic
Consciousness delivers

Becoming there to the will
Of The Unknown God.

So
The old man triumphs
With his blessed assurance.

Then
He gives thanks.

Into trance drove mind
Of the artist seeking beauty
And the essence of beauty.

He found
The essential character
Of things in themselves
To surface
As his third eye looked
Into the unknown.

Faithful; to the phantom
His muse
He pyramided
Into the deep touch
Where he imaged
Being and nothingness
As the tension
Between what was

And the shadow
Of what was.

To build
A testament
Based on hidden meaning
The artist formulated
A two-dimensional reality
Into the life and breath
Of becoming there.

Escaping from the linear
He projected himself
From a parabola of time
Into the beyond
Through a portal
To Truth.

How
The calculus
Of time and spaced
Triggered
A vision of a worker
Alone in a vast sea
Of gold.

The wind crossed the field
As a crow
Battled with the breath
Of death.

Then
The artist looked
To the shadows
As the moment depicted
Times and a half.

So
The artist felt
An awakening
That took him
Onto cosmic consciousness
And the essence of beauty
Trumpeted forevermore.

So
There is connectivity
Between beauty, Truth
And cosmic consciousness.

To see
Into what is there
Releasing the substance
Of time and space
The artist reaches
The authentic article
Through being and nothingness.

It is
The mystery of life

That he pictures
The essence
Of times and a half.

Then
The phantom aligns
The juxtaposition of forms
Into connectivity
Beyond the here and now
And the artist
Takes a leap of faith
Into the unknown.

To be
At the edge
Where Truth begins
He builds an edifice
Of meaning
From across the horizon
Of what matters.

Then
Appearing as a crew
The phantom issues
A call to becoming there
And the artist carves color
Into hidden meaning.

It is
The formulation
Of what is there
With Truth

And the call
To mind and heart
That pronounces ventures
Into the unknown
As the crow carries life
As the artist indwells
Pure music.

There is
The mystery of self
Overpowering
Outliving self
As the artifact of forevermore
Pyramids
Into the dance of the crow
In an endless sky.

Although
The heart and mind
Of the artist sees Truth
Through becoming there
The dull round shadows
The essential substance
Of being and nothingness.

To witness
The movement
Of the celestial clocks
As the lights of the heavens

Show the way
To the authentic article
The artist unearths
The breath of life
From the close at hand.

Then
Liberated from the clutches
Of self-deception
Mind takes heart
Into the juxtaposition
Of things in themselves
And the deep touch
Applies connectivity.

From there
A leap of faith designs
What matters.

Because the image of Truth
Trumps dasein
As a portal to the beyond
Allows passage
To a vertical column of time
The artist reaches
Cosmic consciousness
Through meditation.

Then
Pure music pours
Into heart
And the rhythm

Of the deep touch
Carries mind
Across the expanse.

Then
The artist pictures
The elements
Of a moment
When times and a half
Penetrate forevermore
However
It is the always
Already there
That speaks to heart
As the workings
Of blessed assurance
Reveal The Unknown God.

Once there
The third eye beholds eternity.

So
Linear time and space
Govern the biological clock
And the cup of the artist
Overflows.

To pursue beauty
The artist configures

An image
Beyond space and time
As the phantom
Draws meaning and purpose
Into what is there.

It is
The workings
Of cosmic consciousness
That extends the moment
Into an epiphany
Thus, releasing the substance
Of hidden meaning.

Standing tall
Among a wilderness
Of ideas
The artist gives
What is there
A celebration of life
As it is
When reaching the beyond
Through the substance
Of the close at hand.

As the given
Precedes becoming there
The artist portrays
The always already there
With the power
Of the deep touch

And an image leaps
Out of linear time and space.

Far into a two-dimensional
Reality
He travels into a portal
To the cosmic clock
And a vertical column of time
Allows him knowledge
Of the mystery of life.

Then
The phantom awakens mind
To a slice of another reality
And the artist
Measures what is there
With a vision
Through a looking glass.

Probing
The domain of forevermore
He signifies the beauty
Resident in the minute
Particular
A scene from becoming there.

So
The mystery
In what matters
Presents itself
As pure music
The look of Truth.

As I limped
Through the abyss
Where nothingness filled
Times, the ache of dasein
Confounded mind
With trembling.

It was
Wave upon wav
Of desolation
That bogged down self
As the heart heaved
A breath of no return
And my eyes closed
To all and everything
Blinded by the pain.

When the wind of infamy
Broke thoughts
My bones shattered
And my blood dried.

There seemed no way
Around the moment
As I fell
Through time and space.

Consumed
By the dull round

I could not believe
This pain of dasein
Inflicted upon me
As the shadows
Of tribulation
Encompassed me.

Then
I imaged a crow
In the distance
And it flew into my heart
As the bells
Of cosmic time rang hope
Into the moment.

I felt
An uplifting
As I opened my eyes
To the radiance
Of a figure
And I saw the persona
Of pure music.

It was the phantom.

It was
The signature of hope.

It was
The deep touch
Of The Unknown God.

So it was
That the possible
Nearly became
The close at hand
Accepted
As the way of life
And the tyranny
Of the puppet masters
Surpassed understanding
Yet
The patriots
As a lover of freedom
Stood among the few
Armed with the passion
For Truth,

Although
The war of words
Confounded the air
The patriots listened
To their own heart
And the earth of Truth.

With counterfeit language
The puppet masters tried
To deceive the people
With the desire
To rule the age
But the patriots

Had minds of their own
Believing in liberty and justice.

As a new sun rose
Across the land
The people awoke
To the threat
Against their human rights
And thunder broke
Across the mind
Of becoming there.

Then
The sky opened
And the blood
Of the patriot spoke
To the land
Of the free and brave.

Then
The puppet masters retreated
Into darkness
The place
Where they came from
And the people celebrated
Across the land
Seeing through the deception
Of the age.

So
The war of words ended

And the people lived on
In freedom.

In the garden
Of tables and chairs
Spirits gather
And crows feed them
With indelible thoughts.

It is
A time filled
With pure music
And the rhythm of drums
Leads to the deep touch.

Although
The trumpets of the always
Already there
Pronounce the entrance
To forevermore
The dull round retreats
Into a mask
Of self-deception.

There is
Silence in the heart of dasein.

Then
The spirits speak

Truth into the moment
But the traffic
Descends into darkness.

Although
Dasein chooses
To be deaf and blind
To the Truth
Becoming there
Chosen by The Worde
Continues on and on.

For those
Who accept the gift
From The Unknown God
Eternity welcomes them
With the promise
Of pure music
Onto forevermore.

Then
The spirits dance
With the phantom
To the rhythm
Of the cosmic clock
As becoming there
Witnesses the celebration
Emanating
From pure music.

Although
The crows issue

The message of hope
Dasein collapses
Under its own weight
As becoming there
Pyramids into eternity
Along with the spirits
With a trace left
In the garden
Of tables and chairs.

To see
Into the horizon
Where light turns
Darkness into hope
How
A leap of faith
Finds Truth
In the valley
Of forevermore.

Although
Times and a half pass
In silence
An age of chaos rages
And a patriot
Stands watch in the land
Of the free and brave.

When
The celestial clocks
Approach the hour
Of infamy
The patriot remains
Steadfast
With the conviction
Of liberty in his heart.

To fight the good fight
His vision clears
The way for Truth
And justice to reign.

When
The juxtaposition of events
Empties thought of certainty
The patriot connects
The moment
To the entrance of eternity
In the life
Of becoming there.

Then
Vigilant, he releases
The power
Of the everlasting
And dreams of freedom
For all explode
Into a new reality.

To live
And let live
Is his doctrine
As the lives
Of liberty conquer
Oppression.

It is
In the heart of the patriot
To preserve and protect
One nation under
The Unknown God
Onto forevermore.

In the backlands of mind
Where the wilderness
Reaches the sky
The artist proclaims
The purpose of beauty
And Truth registers
The destiny of what matters.

It is
In the look of becoming there
As the third eye
Pictures the substance
Of the close at hand
That the artist reaches

Into the splendor
Of pure music.

Then
With the deep touch
He trances
Into another reality
Toppling the governance
Of the dull round
And seeking the indwelling
Of cosmic consciousness.

Approaching the river
Of life
He extends time and space
Into a moment
Beyond the given
As he deciphers
Hidden meaning.

Then
The wind bears witness
To a leap of faith
Into the unknown
As the phantom lights
The way to Truth
And the fearsome symmetry
Of things in themselves
Connects image
To a wondrous mystery.

To stand
On the earth of being
And picture
The other side of time
And space
The artist passes
Through a portal
To the beyond
As trumpets sound
The beginning
Of what matters.

It is
Through the trance
That the artist
Unleashes the secrets
Of life.

From the light
In her eyes
The old man saw purpose
And the bedrock
Of the universe
Spoke Truth to his heart.

It was
Tantamount to the thoughts
Of the sages
The fundamental belief

In the message
From cosmic consciousness.

He saw
A purpose in her look
That revealed true beauty
The grace of her walk
Bringing the deep touch
Of the everlasting.

How
Smiling eyes disclosed
An expanse of wonder
And the old man
Held a vision of pure music.

Then
The phantom raised
The moment
Onto a parabola of time
And she joined
Becoming there
To the celestial clocks
As time and space
Flew beyond the possible.

So
The purpose of beauty
Connected the now points
To destiny
As one breath led
To another

And the old man
Kissed the stars.

Then
A warm rain awoke
Becoming there
To her substance
As the treasures
Of pure music poured
The rhythm of eternity
Into his form.

So
The light in her eyes
Revealed the purpose
Of beauty
As Truth indwelled
In the heart of the old man.

So
Beauty is its purpose In itself
As a given.

Plunging further into trance
The old man saw
The approach of a figure
Glowing white
As he looked back
To times and a half.

There was
The aura of triumph
To the moment
As majesty shone
Through Truth
And the old man
Turned to The Word.

As he reached
Into a parabola of time
The figure towered
Into the sky
And the old man voyaged
Into the beyond.

Then
Pure music filled
The air with splendor
And the figure shone
Ever brighter
With aa robe shining.

Through this figure
A portal opened
And the old man tasted
The breath of becoming there.

It was that
The blood of the lamb
Redeemed
All of time and he felt

The treasure
Of blessed assurance.

Then
The mask of self-deception
Crumbled
As the authentic article
Spirited him
With Truth and he advanced
Onto forevermore.

Because
This immaculate figure
Held promise
In the moment
The old man trusted
The deep touch
Of The Unknown God
And the seas
Of the always already there
Stirred with passion.

Because it was
A calling to his heart
And mind
That eclipsed dasein
The substance
Of the given fulfilled
The life of the old man.

Section 6
Footprints of a Parabola of Time

As the phantom
Liberates time
And times and a half
The artist approaches
Pure music
With the will to be.

To depict the heart
Of things in themselves
He calls
Upon the phantom
To trace the architecture
Of the moment.

Then
From behind the dull round
She delivers the domain
Of hidden meaning

And the artist pursues
The elements of being
And nothingness.

Their bond
Surpasses understanding
As they travel
Through the unknown
With visions of Truth.

There is
The rhythm
Of the cosmic clock
In their look
As the substance
Of becoming there configures
A leap of faith.

Then
The root of what is there
Grows into the image
Of time and space
With the deep touch
Of the authentic article
And the artist bleeds Truth
Into images of thought.

So
Heart pursues freedom
As mind calculates
The dimensions of possibility.

So
An image appears
In the looking glass
Of the always already there
And it pyramids
Into a vertical column
Of time.

With the phantom
The artist depicts
The passage of becoming there
Into the mystery of life
As the third eye sees
Through pure music.

Meditating on The Word
I empty my mind
Of troubles
As my heart pounds with life.

As The Unknown God
Reaches me
With the deep touch
The sound of pure music
In the air carries me
Far into the beyond.

Beneath
Things in themselves

The parody
Of the dull round
Incites the feeling
That the world
Is too much with me.

Then
I open the third eye
To what matters.

Although
My breath labors
For becoming there
The gift of life prospers
Toward eternity
As the moment
Eclipses outliving self.

Then
A crow lands
On my shoulder
And speaks of the peace
Beyond understanding.

The message resonates
In my bones.

When
Times and a half
Of the past bleed
Through mind
The expanse registers

The redeeming of time
Forevermore.

Infused with splendor
Becoming there accepts
A bounty of goodness
And the moment
Empowers the breath
With the everlasting
In the heart.

To believe in The Word
Magnifies my life and I praise
The Unknown God for the life
I have been given.

To be thankful liberates mind.

Recounting times
When folly grasped me
How
My wayward ways
Crippled mind
Biting down hard
On whom I was
But
I have left that tyranny
Finding peace in The Word.

In the lone of my time
Becoming there prospers
In the will
Of The Unknown God.

Although
I can do nothing
To change the past
I can learn
The ways of righteousness
And follow Truth.

Although
It is hard
To forgive myself
Although
The past haunted me
I found forgiveness
In The Word.

So
The Truth has set me free.

It was
The power of the deep touch
That moved my heart
Toward forgiveness
Although my mind grieved.

So
All have sinned
And fall short

Of the glory
Of The Unknown God.

To leave
The ways of dasein
Where self-deception ruled
Becoming there awoke
'to the way
The Truth and the life.

So
I have learned
Not to cast the first stone
And live and let live.

As becoming there
Drinks in pure music
I meditate on the gift
Of faith in The Word.

To celebrate life
In the living moment
How
Eternity opens
The mind of becoming there.

There is
The treasure
Of blessed assurance

And the will
Toward the authentic
Article
That brings the breath
Of Truth
Into times and a half.

So
He followed the dance
Of the phantom
Onto a parabola of time
And the spiritual energy
Of the given carried him
Onto pure music.

It was
The deep touch
Of cosmic consciousness
That married him
To a vertical column of time
And the moment
Allowed him to see
Through a looing glass
Onto forevermore.

Placing a promise
In his heart
The phantom allowed him
To pursue the unknown
Through a portal
Onto possibility.

So
She allowed him
To enter trance, guiding him
Through the substance
Of phenomenal reality
And the always
Already there gave him
Horizons beyond the horizon.

Then
The moment painted
The light of Truth
Among the shadows.

Then
Mind weighed
Being and nothingness.

So
Nothingness exists
In the province of mind
As despair.

So
The phantom liberated him
From the cage of self-deception.

As the biological clock
Drives linear time

Into a three
Dimensional reality
Becoming there seeks
The earth that matters
From the here and now
Of possibility.

It was
Through the phantom
That he learned
How the trance offered a way
To the unknown, revealing secrets
Held by hidden meaning.

As he looked
Through a looking glass
The deep touch brought him
Onto another place
And time and space
Moved into a two
Dimensional reality.

Then
He felt the nearness
Of cosmic consciousness
As his mind leaped
Through a portal
To a horizon of horizons.

It was
The power of a vertical
Column of time

That spoke a wilderness
Of thought
As he climbed
Out of himself.

Then
The juxtaposition
Of the elements
Of phenomenal reality
Brought things
In themselves
Into his presence
And he connected
What was there to Truth.

How
Being on the outside
Of time and space
Triggered a vision
Onto forevermore
As the phantom traced
The way
The Truth and the life
Into his heart.

Then
He believed
The Unknown God.

To unearth
Hidden meaning and to probe
The unknown
How
The mystery of being
And nothingness fogs
The apprehension
Of things in themselves.

Engendering a leap of faith
The grammar of becoming there
Allows the artist
To envision the substance
Of what matters
Through the deep touch.

It is
Seeing to and indwelling
With the beyond
That takes the artist
Into the light of life
And the phantom fills him
With a passion for Truth.

Appearing in the wilds of mind
An image surfaces
And the artist pictures
Pure music.

Following the rhythm
Of the celestial clocks
Becoming there edges

Ever closer
To the rubric of time and space
As raw splendor
Writes itself
Into the movement
Of the authentic article.

Then
The breath of life infuses
Connectivity into a vision.

Then
The phantom carries
The artist
Into an epiphany
Unearthing possibility.

Then
The phantom unearths
Hidden meaning
And she presents
The deep touch
Onto the artist.

To be
With the living moment
Releases the binds
Of the linear
And an image breathes
In a life of itself.

With the breath of life
Linear time and space
Measure
The beginning and end
To heart and mind
As dasein resides
In self-deception.

How
Being the center
Of all and everything
Is the rubric
Of bad faith
As the conduct
Of becoming there proves
As true and right.

It is not
Trusting self
But believing
In a higher order
That allows the approach
To the unknown
For trust determines
The foundation of life.

Dedicated
To a sense of duty
Becoming there

Has no beginning or end
As belief joins sacrifice
To the always already there.

So
There is war
And there always is war
As becoming there serves
Destiny
As the last man standing.

There is
No greater war
Than the war in mind
A universal conflict
From beginning to end.

There is
No greater peace
Than the mind at peace
As heart echoes
Life everlasting.

So
Becoming there follows
The rhythm of pure music
As a triumph
Over oppression
And the battle cry
For freedom
Transcends time and space.

So
There is virtual Truth
And veritable Truth.

As the bones of eternity
Dance in the wilds of mind
And pure music moves
The muscle of heart
Becoming there joins
The rhythm of Truth
And blessed assurance
Fills moments with wonder.

However
Burying the self
Through the distortion
Of time and space
Dasein consumes itself
As an existential breach.

So
Dasein buries possibility
Blind to the way
That matters
Because it breathes
With self-deception.

There is
The pain of being

And nothingness
A burden heavy
Upon the heart
And a despair that cripples
The mind.

There is
No dignity in suffering
When the deep touch
Triggers hope
As self turns
Its back on Truth
As The Word calls
Upon the spirit.

So
There is no
Greater treasure
Than being in the presence
Of The Unknown God
But dasein listens
To the call of darkness.

Running life
Into the void
Bathing self in dread
Dasein prides itself
With pain endured
Wallowing in bad faith.

Then
The Word speaks Truth

Into the heart
And becoming there
Triumphs over dasein
Because life is
To be toward
The everlasting.

So
Faith is the resurrection
Of ideation
And knowledge is
The experiential
Based on the optics
Of phenomenal reality.

Where knowledge ends, faith begins.

Then
In the garden
Of tables and chairs
Where spirits gathered
I saw the phantom
And she was beautiful.

Speaking Truth
Into the moment
She pulled me
Into the presence
Of cosmic consciousness

And my mind opened
To a vertical column of time.

Pure music is there
As the pounding rhythm
Of always and forever
While the phantom
Presses time into space.

Across the horizon
The spirits capture
Shadows of Truth
As the deep touch
Carries mind
Into celestial dynasties.

As I traveled
Further into trance
A chorus of spirits
Followed the phantom
Into things in themselves
And veritable Truth
Shone with the light
Of forevermore.

Then
From the here and now
The dull round
Composed a message
Carving it
Into the heart of being
And nothingness

But it lacked
The authentic article.

The phantom marked it
As virtual Truth.

So
The mind-speak
Of the world, motivated
By self-indulgence
Is virtual Truth
While veritable Truth
Comes from the deep touch.

So
There is a war between
Being and nothingness.

When the dawn of thought
Issued a passageway
To the thing in itself
Mind awoke
To the battle
Between principalities.

It was
The juxtaposition
Of forms and substances
Within the here and now

That prompted visions
Along the way
To nothingness.

Then
Hidden meaning
Behind the close at hand
Surfaced before
The third eye of trance
As connectivity joined
The authentic article
To becoming there.

So
Faith conquered the doubts
Occupying dasein
As the hypothesis
Of life proved possible.

Looking
Into the eyes of nothingness
Feeling the stir of despair
Becoming there eclipsed
Outliving self
And the heart
Of cosmic consciousness
Echoed in the breath
Of principalities.

To be
Beyond self allowed
Mind to follow

Pure music
To veritable Truth
As the phantom
Indwelled
Cosmic consciousness.

It is
That cosmic consciousness
Allows mind to leap
Into the living moment
And nothingness recedes
Into darkness.

Then
There is peace
In the harvest of thought.

In the darkness sirens scream
And life goes on.

Somewhere
Tragedy strangles life.

To live
At the edge of the abyss
Where death knocks
At the door
How frail
This thing called life

As linear time devours
Times and a half.

For dasein
Absence is a myth
As nothingness surrounds
The living moment
While becoming there
Prepares
For the everlasting.

To live
As a stranger
To possibility
Dasein closes its eyes
To destiny.

Then
The bells of eternity
Chime the hour
And the mind busies itself
With shuffling of feet
A shortness of breath
And a shrug of shoulders.

So
There will come a time
When i join
The no longer
But my belief
In The Word takes me

Into a peace
Beyond understanding.

I am here to serve
The Unknown God
And I know
Death shall have
No dominion.

To have
Blessed assurance
Is to be
With pure music
That teaches the way
The Truth and the life.

As the artist
Stares at the blank canvas
The phantom liberates
Time and space
As colors radiate
The shadows
Of being and nothingness.

In the substance
Of a thought
Mind imagines
A virtual Truth
As the freedom

Of becoming there
Opens a vision
To the mystery and wonder
Of hidden meaning.

There is
At first uncertainty
A hesitant look
At what matters
Until the deep touch
Carries an image
That depicts the dynamic
Of the moment.

Then
An order of a thing
In-itself coalesces
And the artist bathes
In the pure music
Of the everlasting.

So
There is eternity
In the vison.

So
There is an epiphany
To the vision.

Then
The blank canvas
Comes alive

With the heart beat
That drives
Time and space.

Then
The deep touch
connects
Color to form
As mind travels
Into the unknown.

So
The artist draws
Breath from the veritable Truth
Based on the experiential
As the phantom yields
The substance of the message.

Then
Cosmic consciousness
Colors shadows
Of being and nothingness
As the infusion
Of a vertical column of time
Empowers
The artist with awe.

In the wilderness of thought
Where mind seeks

The unknown
A river of ideas reflects
The dance of the phantom
And times and a half
Flow to eternity.

Among the underbrush
Of ideation
Becoming there looks
To the close at hand
For veritable Truth
But all is covered
By hidden meaning.

Then
The third eye pursues trance
And the river comes alive.

Then
An epiphany rises
From the earth
And pure music pours
Wonder from the sky.

Because
The deep touch
Extends mind
With the rub
Of possibility
Becoming there pyramids
The length and breadth
Of what is there

As the bells of forevermore
Awaken the bones
Of the here and now.

As the wilderness connects
Mind to the song of the everlasting
The unknown trumpets
The thing-in-itself.

As the substance
Of what matters
Echoes across the hills
The river gives up
The living moment.

Because times and a half
Flow with the passion
Of the dance
And will drives into the treasures
Of the always already there
The veritable Truth centers
Upon the magnitude
Of possibility.

So
The Unknown God lives.

Where there is possibility
There is opportunity.

Although
Nothingness creeps
Into the moment
And the abyss consumes
The he that he had become
Leaving shadows of a life
The phantom intervenes
Within times and a half
Until his heart
Finds a way to endure.

The existential horizon
Of being and nothingness
Withers mind
But
Pure music filters
Through time and space
Issuing hope
In another day.

So
The boundaries
Of becoming there
Allow the will
To pyramid
Into what maters
As the phantom
That owns into him
Opens possibility.

To be chosen
As a child

Of The Unknown God
Expands the horizon
Into the far reaches
Of thought
And then into the beyond
Where self joins
The way
The Truth and the life.

So
Becoming thee
Is being toward veritable Truth
Ever reaching for pure music.

Then
The rhythm
Of the cosmic clock
Releases the chains of dasein
As the phantom brings the deep
Touch, allowing access
To the wilderness of ideation.

So
Hope is a most wondrous gift.

There is
A mystery tree
That glows in the dark
A tree of gold

And precious stones
That speaks treasures
In the wind.

Beneath its boughs
A man gathers thought
And eternity stirs
The bones of becoming there.

In a moment of Truth
Times and a half
Reveal a portal
To the beyond
As trance takes him
Into the center
Of things-in-themselves.

Then
The authentic article
Encompasses him
And he breathes in
Life everlasting.

Then
A crow brings his mind
Into a place of wonder
And he sees the way
The Truth and the life.

Among the bones
Of this mystery tree
The language of what

Matters most
Deciphers hidden meaning
As pure music fills the sky
With trumpets of glory.

Then
Cosmic consciousness
Allows the moment
To pyramid life
As the deep touch
Summons an epiphany
And becoming there walks
Into forevermore.

Then
The crow turns itself
Into the phantom
As she intercedes
Between being and nothingness.

On the mystery tree
A life is given
And The Unknown God
Adopts the man
Into a harvest of souls.

Into the mix
With the indwelling
Of the always already there

The artist is thrown
And worlds collide
Unleashing the power
Of things-in-themselves
Until the image
Of time and space reveal
A passage into nonbeing
a coalescing through trance.

As mystery fills the moment
Of the deep touch
The artist draws life
Into a two
Dimensional reality
And the phantom awakens
The veritable Truth
In his heart.

Then
He turns to the rhythm
From pure music
And the drums
Of eternity sound
Thunder into mind.

Then
Nonbeing frees
The substance
Of what is there
As the flow of possibility
Forms an image
Behind thought.

Feeling his way
Through the unknown
The artist fathoms
Being and nothingness
Working that idea
Into a step through
The beyond.

It is
From the other sisde
Of what is there
That nonbeing gathers
The moment
Launching becoming there
Into a leap of faith/

Then
The phantom rubs life
Into his form
And she projects
Veritable Truth
Through his vision.

Dismissing
The constraints
Of linear time and space
The artist portrays
The reaches
Of things-in-themselves.

It is
That becoming there
Through trance
Signifies as nonbeing
A posture
Of climbing outside self.

Nonbeing presents itself
Outside of linear time and space
Onto a parabola of time
And access to a portal
To the beyond.

Meditating on The Word
Becoming there probes
The unknown
In pursuit of Truth.

So
Becoming there dwells
In pure music
An epiphany pyramiding
Through being and nothingness
Gathering thought
And finding a vision
Of the given.

Although
Nonbeing is beyond
The here and now
There is an anchor
In the close at hand

Offering a touchstone
To the thing-in-itself.

Through the deep touch
From The Unknown God
Becoming there traverses
Possibility, as the wilderness
Of mind and heart
Finds the peace
Beyond understanding.

Then
Nonbeing is equipped
And ready
For the war of principalities.

Armed with Truth
Becoming there battles
The frontier
Known as the dull round
All those who choose
An ugly life.

Through trance
Becoming there unearths
Hidden meaning
As the phantom lights
The lamp of eternity
With her dance
A persona of the crow.

To probe the unknown
Undressing hidden meaning
Becoming there erases
The mask of dasein
And rubs life with nonbeing
Through meditation.

Behind the mask of dasein
Deception bleeds into life
And bad faith spreads rancor.

To be true
To The Word allows
Becoming there the vision
Of the other side
Of time and space
Following the dance
Of the phantom
As she unearths
Being and nothingness.

The destiny of dasein
Is to outlive self
And be a tragedy
In the death
Of the moment.

As nonbeing prospers
In the search of Truth

An island of hope
Appears in the drift
Of the always already there
And the phantom leads
Becoming there
To cosmic consciousness
Through the deep touch.

Then
The character
Of what matters indwells
The moment.

Then
Eternity opens the way
To The Unknown God.

Entering the domain
Of the cosmic clock
Becoming there rises
Outside of self
And reaches the everlasting
As the phantom trumpets
Pure music.

Then
Becoming there goes
The way of Truth in life.

As nonbeing traversed
The interstices of mind
An image appeared
One of pure music.

It was
An epiphany in time
And space
Juxtaposed with the always
Already there
That took becoming there
Into an anthem of glory
Where the phantom
Danced into forevermore.

Plunging into the unknown
Nonbeing broke
The mask of self
Deception
To indwell with the dynamic
Of the authentic article
As the phantom
Connected becoming there
To a parabola of time.

There was
The movement into trance
That allowed a moment
In the wilderness of thought
To proclaim freedom
Before the walls
Of the unknown

And the celestial clocks
Signaled a time to be.

Then
Becoming there launches
Into the shadows
Of being and nothingness.

Then
Phenomenal reality
Falls into the shadows
Of time and space.

Suddenly
Presence appeared
In the garden
Of tables and chairs
        Where becoming there
Unearthed hidden meaning
As the third eye
Probed the drift of life.

It is
An existential moment.

It is
An epiphany of time and space.

It is
The pure music of eternity.

It was
The beauty of pure music
That swept across
Time and space
That awoke
Nonbeing to becoming there.

What was there
Trumpeted freedom
Into the blood
Of the living
As the moment rolled
Into being and nothingness
A conflict of mind.

As thought sought
The moment
The rise of the unknown
Brought the dawn
Of times and a half
Because the trance had brought
The mystery of life
Into full view.

When the void trampled
The beginning
Of the close at hand
Becoming there
Turned to The Word

With faith
As the guiding light.

How
Eternity spoke
Through the living moment
Unearthing the way
To Truth and life
As the phantom
Armed with love
Brought hope
To the wasteland.

Although
The tyranny
Of self-deception hungered
For the heart
Of becoming there
The deep touch
Of The Unknown God
Would lose
None of the children
Of faith.

Although
The struggle for Truth
Labored
Times and a half
Pure music took
Becoming there
To hallowed ground.

Then
The Word gave
Blessed assurance
To becoming there.

SECTION 7
LOOKING GLASS

So
The third eye is
The looking glass
Of the soul.

Riding wild
Through a wilderness
Of time and space
The patriot chased destiny
Down the asphalt ribbon.

It is
That the road
And the patriot are one.

It is
That the ride
And eternity are one.

To follow

The celestial dynasties
Into the wonder
Of nonbeing
Leaving the center of self
For the beyond
The patriot harvested
The vast fields of Truth
Finding an oasis
In the heart
Of becoming there.

So
He stopped at the garden
Of tables and chairs
In full view
Of the blue ridge mountains.

Among the spirits there
The patriot sat
As mind eclipsed
Outliving self
And self-deception died
In the distant past.

The mask
Of bad faith belonged
To the no longer
As he groomed himself
With pure music.

The spirits raised
His vision of the world

To cosmic consciousness
When the phantom
Opened his third eye.

Then
The rhythm of the way
To Truth and life
Signaled his destiny
Because the patriot belonged
To The Unknown God.

Mounting the deep touch
Of his iron thunder
He blazed the road
With blessed assurance.

Born to be
The artist lives Truth.

So
The artist followed the moon
Along the river
Into the interior of time and space
As mind traversed
The unknown.

Where becoming there reached
The limits of its time
The artist leaped

Into pure music
Orchestrating beauty
With the spirits
Of the always already there.

It was
A warm and fluid time.

It was
The deep touch
Of cosmic consciousness.

Then
The phantom spirited
A moment
With the celestial dynasties
As destiny formed
The substance of life.

She danced to the rhythm
Of the cosmic clock
That spoke to her heart
As the artist planted
The image of forevermore.

With power and might
The artist brushed hidden meaning
Into what was there
As moon shadows conveyed
The drift of the thing-in-itself.

Triggered by the deep touch

The artist pulled
The authentic article
Into an image that belonged
To another side
Of time and space
As the phantom pated
The moon with blood.

Casting the moment
With the flow of the river
The artist flew meaning
On the wings of the moon
As the unknown
Flourished with life.

Beneath the blue sky
Thoughts stir
As mind looks
At being and nothingness.

Triggered by the wind
An image broke
Upon becoming there
That lifted the third eye
To the spaces
Of the always already there.

Then
Bells chimed the hour

When Truth appeared
In the close-at-hand
And the substance
Of what mattered
Surged hungry
For pure music.

Accelerating
Into time and space
Becoming there passed
Possibility
Approaching life
Between the mask
Of dasein
And the thing-in-itself.

Because of the divide
Of being and nothingness
Dasein writhes
In bad faith
Wallowing in despair.

It was
The presence of thee unknown
That brought times
And a half into view.

It is
The rhythm of a parabola
Of time that takes
Mind through a portal
To the essence

Of the existential moment
As thought invades
The province
Of hidden meaning.

Then
The phantom shook
The light of day
Filling mind with images
As the third eye
Took meditation
Into a song of silence.

So
The impossible became
The inevitable
Through hidden meaning.

So
The source of pure music
Is beyond the blue sky.

It was
A simple choice:
To accept the way
To Truth and life
Or be buried
With the contempt
Of dasein.

It was
The existential moment
When the mask
Of self-deception dissolved
In inner space
And dasein lurked
In the shadows
Of being and nothingness.

Reaching into nonbeing
Through trance
Becoming there indwells
The deep touch
And eternity lights
With pure music.

Rubbing thought
With possibility
Nonbeing ventures
Into the unknown
Searching
For hidden meaning
As becoming there
Experiences
A leap of faith.

Then
The channels
To what matters
Fills the third eye
With visions
Of another kind.

So
The other side
Of time and space
Pictures veritable reality
Through the deep touch
As nonbeing penetrates
The always already there.

It is
That becoming there
Is thrown
Into time and times
And a half
Finding life
As the experiential
Gathers thought
Toward meaning.

As the phantom
Delivers pure music
Nonbeing spirits the way
To The Unknown God
Through meditation
On The Word.

Between the spaces
Of times and a half
Beauty forms
In the frontier of moments

Triggered by the rustlings
Of pure music.

Before
There was anything else
There was the pulse
Of cosmic consciousness
Speaking into the substance
Of the always already there
A rhythm of Truth
Flowing across possibility.

So
Beauty emerges
From the deep touch
That breathes in
Nothingness
And breathes out Truth.

There
In the wind of eternity
The Unknown God forms
The symmetry of time and space
As the wonder
Of origins celebrates
Becoming there
With an epiphany
Of forevermore.

Along the way
Nonbeing stirred
Into the third eye

And through the third eye
Beauty and Truth
Were one
As the message
That conveyed meaning
To the heart
Of becoming there.

It was
That beauty tickled
A body of Truth.

It was
The anatomy of Truth
That rubbed life
Into becoming there.

So
Beauty is the doorway
To Truth.

So
Pure music is
The looking glass to the beauty
Of forevermore.

Then
A day ended
As the visit

267

To the other side
Of time and space
And the artist gathered Truth
From the substance
Of the close at hand.

It was
The pure music
Of the always already there
That took him
Into a wilderness
Of times and a half
As the third eye
Probed the unknown.

When
The mystery of hidden meaning
Surfaced
The artist drew the breath
Of nonbeing
And mountains
Of the everlasting rose
From heart.

Then
The phantom took him
Into the war of principalities
Where nothingness battled
Against being
Until life defined
The moment of Truth.

So
The phantom showed him
The authentic article
That spoke
Through the triumph
Of the everlasting.

There was
The tremor
Of the mountains
As heart configured
The substance
Of that which was
Cast in the wind.

So
The phantom showed him
The elements of dasein
And how it outlived self
As becoming there
Drank in the dynamic
Of forevermore.

Then
The day ended
With the peace
Beyond understanding.

Time and times
And a half pass
As mind pursues Truth
And thoughts spin
With cosmic consciousness.

When the dawn
Of all and everything
Surpassed understanding
The quick of becoming there
Leaped toward the presence
Of The Unknown God
And Truth became
The face of pure music.

It was
Through meditation
That the third eye
Reckoned life
As the passage
To the everlasting
And the breath
Of the living moment
Triggered the mystery
Of what mattered.

How
The heart of becoming there
Pounds possibility
Into the substance
Of the close at hand.

Then
The phantom speaks
Nonbeing into becoming there
As the authentic article
Saturates the moment
With blessed assurance.

There is
No self-deception.

There is
Only Truth and the beauty
Of what was meant to be.

So
The purpose of life
Endures as pure music.

Then
Nonbeing listens
To the anthem
Of forevermore
And the third eye
Pyramids becoming there
Toward the light
Of the always already there.

Then
Nonbeing experiences
The Word
As the living Truth.

To be
A free spirit
Through the oppression
Of the dull round
How
The angels sing
An anthem of glory
And times celebrate
The gift of wonder.

To live
Through hard times
But not to be buried
By despair
How
The life of a free spirit
Triumphs over adversity
As the dull round
Recedes into the void.

In the meadow
Of times and a half
The free spirit gathers thought
As mind reflects
The glow of eternity
And heart basks
In the radiance of forevermore.

There is
No darkness in a free spirit.

It is
The liberty
Of becoming there
That advances presence
Into the mystery
Of this thing called life
As mind thrives
With the breath
Of life.

To look
Into the eyes of the abyss
And conquer the depths
Of despair
Becoming there turns
To The Unknown God
And tribulation
Passes away

It is
That a leap of faith
Allows a free spirit
To be.

It is
Through the deep touch
Of The Word
That allows

The free spirit
To be.

It is
Through the deep touch
Of The Word
That allows the free spirit
To live a life
Of pure music.

To take with the crows
To speak their language
To know their thoughts
How
The spirit
Of the thing-in-itself
Transcends cognition
As I connect the will to be
To the understanding
Of time and space.

So
The end points
Of here and now
And there and then
Breach the limits
Of thought
As the crow
Consumes possibility

And I weather
The drought of dasein.

How
The experiential
Equips mind to fathom
The living moment
In terms
Of the flight of the crow
While I nest
In the garden
Of tables and chairs.

The distance
Between the crow and me
Ranges in the distance
Between me
And cosmic consciousness
As a higher order
Speaks curiosity
Into the moment.

It is
When becoming there
Reaches nonbeing
Through trance
That veritable reality
Fashions perception
Into pure music
Allowing me
To leap out of myself.

Then
The crow takes
The moment
Into the language
Of being and nothingness
And the deep touch
Fills me with promise.

So
The spirit of Truth
Translates the presence
Of The Unknown God
Into intelligent design.

Measuring the dynamics
Of beauty
Mind translates
Veritable reality
Into the symmetry
Of the thing-in-itself
As the substance
Of time and space
Speaks certain Truth.

So
To examine beauty
The anatomy
Of what that is
Becoming there projects

Within and under form
To launch nonbeing
Into the subtext
Of what matters.

Then
Language determines
The perception
Of a figure
The architecture
Of being and nothingness
As the trace
Of veritable reality
Carries thought
Between thinking.

How
The spirit of becoming there
The very articulation
Of pure music
Intercedes in the passage
Of the experiential
And time falls
From the celestial clocks
Revealing the destiny
Of certain Truth.

How
Thought transcends mind
As the third eye
Gathers an image
Of the everlasting.

So
Beauty comes outside itself
As the rhythm
Of a parabola of time
Triggers the deep touch
And nonbeing gathers beauty
From the close at hand.

Then
Beauty appears more true
The closer it gets to certain Truth
As the echoes
Of pure music indwell life.

So
Beauty is the substance of life.

The call of the crow
The undressing of Truth
How
The deep touch
Of the everlasting
Defines time past
As I trance
Into the unknown.

There is
A subtle image
Emanating through the fog

And it appears
To be the phantom
My very love.

As mind eclipses
Nothingness
Thought builds
The history of her look
And I follow the traces
Of hidden meaning
With the language
Known to the crow.

Penetrating
What is there
My third eye pyramids
Her form
As the dense fog
Plays with her presence.

Then
The moment triggers
A longing in my heart
A hunger
For time past
And I know her
As the call of the crow.

What
Treasure she is
As she dances
Through memories

As certain Truth overshadows
Time past and I remember her
From long ago.

So
There is beauty in her look.

So
There is substance
In her becoming there.

In my trance
I see her eyes
And I believe
In the everlasting
Of true love.

I remember her well
As certain Truth.

Among the trees
Of the forest
The phantom spirits
Times and a half
And I follow her dance
Mesmerized by her grace.

Then
She calls to my heart

With a voice
Of the everlasting
And the sky opens
To possibility.

How
The deep touch
Of forevermore carries me
Into the beyond
And I read the substance
Of hidden meaning
From a portal
In the unknown.

So
In her becoming there
The mystery
Surrounding life
Pyramids my mind
Into epiphany
And my passion swells.

How
The rhythm of drums
Moves the anatomy
Of what it means to be
As my third eye
Liberates time and space
And dasein withers
In outliving self.

It is
That dasein is the death of hope.

It is
That dasein smashes
The moment
Shearing breath
Onto the no longer
But becoming there
Grows into abundance.

How
The phantom feeds life
With the splendor
Of the wilds
And she connects me
To The Unknown God.

In the presence of The Word
I see certain Truth
And the phantom smiles.

In the center
Of all and everything
The blue guitar
By Picasso pictures
Pure music
And the dull round feels
The vibrations of eternity.

There is
The movement
Of time and space
That penetrates
The living moment
And an old man casts
The passion of becoming there
Into veritable reality
The substance
Of what is.

How
The sound
Of the blue guitar
Resonates with Truth
As the phantom
Takes time beyond
Possibility.

It is
A leap governed
By the celestial clocks
That transcends
The here and now
As the color blue
Defines the mystery of life.

How
The deep touch of blue
Carries thought beyond mind
And becoming there
Reaches toward a portal

To the everlasting
With the rhythm
Of cosmic consciousness.

Then
The phantom dances
Through the looking glass
As what matters colors
The blue guitar
With the feel
Of rare treasures.

So
Hidden meaning surfaces
Through an image
Revealing Truth
In the living moment
And the blue guitar
Echoes in the heart
Of becoming there.

At the dawn of thought
When becoming there
Reaches into possibility
Mind gathers
The close at hand
As a launching point
Into the unknown.

Passing
One milestone after another
I gravitate
Toward a body of Truth
And pure music shines
Through a looking glass
Of time and space.

Then
The freedom of thought
Orchestrates
The form and substance
Of what matters
As I step
Away from being
And nothingness.

It is
That veritable reality
Presents itself
As the entry into the beyond
And the phantom colors
The dull round
With epiphany.

How
The phantom liberates
Light from darkness
As he intrusion
Of possibility takes me
Into the always already there.

Then
The Unknown God speaks
To the heart
And the body of Truth
Feeds me
With life everlasting.

It is
Through The Word
That I journey past
Time present
Into the splendor
Of the living Truth.

As I phase
Into the beyond
The deep touch opens
Veritable reality
To the way, the Truth
And the life
And I leap
Into forevermore.

Trilogy of the muse available online
Reaching the Beyond
Suspending the Muse
Images of Being There

CPSIA information can be obtained
at www.ICGtesting.com
Printed in the USA
LVHW091048131120
671368LV00003B/137

9 781953 791054